CIAO PUSSY!

CIAO PUSSY!

A MEMOIR OF FLORENCE

Susan Kelley

ISBN: 1515176924
ISBN 13: 9781515176923
Library of Congress Control Number: 2015911759
CreateSpace Independent Publishing Platform
North Charleston, South Carolina

Several of these stories have previously appeared in Sarasota Magazine.

Also by Susan Kelley
Real Women Send Flowers
Why Men Commit
Why Men Stray/Why Men Stay
The Second Time Around
I Oprahed

For William
It's all about the journey

And for the extraordinary people of Florence

Contents

Prologue
1
The Adventure Begins
5
They Love Me in Italy
12
Just Do It
17
Our new home
20
Tests
23
Spousal Credits
26
Lisa
29
The Maestro
33
Different Priorities
38

Florence-Florida
46
The Reluctant Florentine
54
9/11
62
Post 9/11
68
Life Goes On
73
Ciao Pussy
77
Amalfi
84
The "Relationship Expert"
94
Buy or Rent?
97
The Expatriates
102
The Lady Garden
123
Primavera
128
Sister Wendy Beckett
137
Russia
146

La Donna da Sardinia
159

The Art of Provence
167

Intermission
177

Our Renaissance
189

At Home in Florence
203

Hemingway and Stresa
209

La Vita Italiana
214

Settling In
224

Massage with Maximilliano
238

The Art of Shoes
243

Florence in the Fall
248

Return to Casali di Bibbiano
262

La Dolce Vita, Florentine Style
269

Giorno del Ringraziamento
276

The Exit Plan
290
Final Thoughts
297
Our Favorite Restaurants, Cafès, Trattorie, and other venues
301
Recipes
305
A Note About the Author
321

Prologue

After landing at the airport in Florence, we load our six suitcases into a taxi and set off through the numerous cobblestone roads. The cab driver navigates his way through the narrow one-way streets and stops in front of massive wooden-arched doors at Lungarno Archibusieri No. 6, next to the Trattoria Ponte Vecchio. We are a middle-aged couple who speak no Italian and who know nobody in the city, standing on the curb with our luggage, exhausted.

We had been told the residence was on the first floor. Bill rings the buzzer, and the door is magically unbolted. It opens to a dark hallway, and I'm thinking this is going to be a dreary apartment. Before us, a steep staircase disappears into shadows. "Allo? Mr. Kelley?" someone calls. The owner, a lovely woman our age, greets us from the top of the stairs. The first floor is the American second floor, we later learn. Our first lesson in Florence real estate. We trudge upward into the unknown.

Every year on a Sunday in late September or early October, the city of Florence gathers for *Corri la Vita* (Run for Life), a 13km competitive race and 5km non-competitive walk for charity, supporting public health facilities specializing in the fight against breast cancer. Now it is held in Piazza Duomo, but in the early years the crowd would assemble in front of the Palazzo Vecchio in Piazza della Signoria under the copy of Michelangelo's *David*. (The original sculpture is housed safely indoors at the Accademia gallery.)

The first time my husband Bill and I participated in this event, we met with new friends, outfitted like ourselves in the official T-shirt, provided by Armani at the time for a modest 10-euro contribution. Staring up at the statue, my husband said, "To my mind, Michelangelo is the greatest artist who ever lived; the combination of his paintings, his sculpture, and his work ethic is unmatched." As we listened intently to his thoughtful assessment of one of the greatest artistic geniuses of all time, he paused, nodded at David, and added with a sly grin, "But mine's bigger."

This festive occasion could be considered our official annual kick-off when we return to Florence each fall and gather with our friends for the walk.

The Adventure Begins

In 1997, my husband made a life-altering decision to sell his successful IT consulting business in order to concentrate full time on his rapidly developing art career. He was and is an artist in his soul, and I supported his decision completely. My writing career was also blossoming with the recent publication of my third book. To celebrate this momentous decision, we planned our first trip to Italy. Bill wanted to paint and I planned to do research for a new book. We decided to focus on Rome, Florence, and Venice, with stops in Tuscany. I had my heart set on a luxurious spa in Montecatini Terme and Bill wanted to go to Anzio, the site of the WWII amphibious landing his father took part in on the day Bill was born. But mainly, we were looking forward to a wonderful month-long vacation together. I promised myself I would pack light. I hit the summer sales with a vengeance and end up with an almost all-Donna Karan wardrobe—midnight blue tops and slacks, cream colored jeans and tees, along with a few black pieces thrown in for good measure. I had just read an article titled, "Look Taller with Monochromatic Dressing."

I went on a crash diet—all protein, no carbohydrates—so I would have room to gain back any accumulated pounds from over-indulgences in wine and pasta. I felt chic, comfortable, and deliriously happy with my cross-body purse and my rubber-soled walking shoes as we embarked on this journey.

Tall, husky, tanned, and impeccably dressed in a pale blue shirt, coordinated tie and dark trousers, Enrico, a driver and guide recommended by a friend, approaches us as we leave the baggage claim area, at Fiumicino airport holding a sign with our name. He puffs out his chest and greets us formally as Signor and Signora Kelley.

Enrico proved to be an amazing and knowledgeable guide. Over the course of our week in Rome he explained the history of Italy and gave us a new understanding of his country. He began each sentence with, "You must understand," sounding exactly like Robert DeNiro. He explained to us that there is really no such thing as Italy. The city-states fought each other for hundreds of years and Italy only became united in 1871, not long after the U.S. Civil War. It is Enrico who, upon finding out our occupations, begins to refer to my husband as *"pittore famoso"* (famous painter) and me as "*scrittore famosa*" (famous writer).

Enrico thinks of himself as a *Roman,* proud of his heritage, not an *Italian.* He tells us that the Italians who moved to America, those we might find in Little Italy, in New York, and the North End, in Boston, were from the south, Sicily and Naples. "Romans, Florentines, Venetians: we stay here," he says.

Proving his value as a guide, he says he can get us behind the scenes at the Vatican (for a substantial price, the equivalent of $800 for two.) We agree, figuring that although pricey, it is a once-in-a-lifetime opportunity.

Several times, I witness money changing hands discretely between Enrico and the Swiss guards as we breeze past queues of tourists. We are led to the balcony where the Pope makes his announcements; visit the famous "crying room," where the newly elected pope reclines on the cream colored chaise and (allegedly) weeps with happiness. We see the smokestack that sends up the white smoke when the new pope is elected and the black smoke when there is still no new pope. We are allowed to enter the Pope's private chapel, the Pauline.

The pope at the time, John Paul II, was Polish and believed in a black Madonna. As we enter this beautiful tiny chapel, we see a bust of the black Madonna on the altar. To our amazement, two of the most famous and priceless frescoes by Michelangelo are there: *The Conversion of St. Paul*, where he is struck by lightning on the road to Damascus, and *The Crucifixion of St. Peter*. Enrico has to practically drag Bill out of the chapel; he stands there, mesmerized, and doesn't want to leave. It is money well spent. Bill wraps his arms around me, dips me back, and we kiss in the pope's private elevator as our guide snaps the photo.

Enrico continues to deliver an insider's tour of The Eternal City, the seat of the Roman Catholic Church, including some of the most sublime art and architecture in the world, as well as Saint Peter's Basilica, the world's largest church built on Vatican Hill. We visit ancient sites like the Colosseum, the Forum, the Catacombs, and Hadrian's Villa, and end the day with a glass of wine in Piazza Navona, gazing on the sublime Bernini fountains. In the next days we visit the Trevi Fountain, the Vatican Museums, Villa Borghese, the Spanish Steps, and Piazza del Popolo.

Enrico drives us to the church of San Pietro in Vincoli (St. Peter in Chains). The church was founded in the fifth century to house the chains that bound St. Peter in Palestine (they're preserved under glass). However, it is best known for the colossal statue of Moses that Michelangelo created for the tomb of Pope Julius II.

One day, on our last stop, Enrico led us to a peek-through view of St. Peter's dome through the keyhole on the gate to the headquarters of the Knights of Malta on Rome's Aventine Hill. As we take turns, we see a garden path that ends with bushes perfectly framing the dome of St. Peter's in the distance.

We return to the city center at day's end and Enrico stops the car to warn us about the gypsies; in that instant, a live demonstration takes place of a pick-pocket in action, only feet from his car.

At night we walk to Piazza della Rotonda, to sit facing the Pantheon, a Roman temple and perhaps the most famous of Rome's ancient sites—almost perfectly preserved despite being built in 126 A.D. Surrounded by small cafes and restaurants, we sip wine at *Scusate il Ritardo* and watch a bent beggar lady draped in black, with her cane and her money cup. We dine at Da Fortunato, the legendary Roman restaurant mentioned in our favorite author, Pat Conroy's novel—*Beach Music*—and discuss the book for the hundredth time.

Enrico is impressed that Bill had done his homework and is so interested in the art and history of Italy. He drives us to Sibilla Restaurant in Tivoli (operating continuously since 1720), on the banks of the Tiber River –in front of Roman temples. After a leisurely lunch, Bill climbs to the top of Tivoli's

Acropolis and poses for my camera, shirtless among the archaic statues.

Bill tells Enrico that we need to go to Anzio, and the next day we head to the coast, a drive that takes a little over an hour. We walk the beach and scoop up a handful of sand to take home with us. Anzio is heartbreaking—like the Normandy beaches—with a huge cemetery of row after row of graves of those who died in battle.

After an intense week in the Eternal City, we embark on a hilarious journey with Enrico, now dressed more casually in yellow golf shirt and blue jeans, which includes an excursion to Assisi. There my outrageous husband is asked to leave the local church after pretending to be a priest hearing the confession of Enrico. The cleric appears and admonishes them in perfect English, saying they should be ashamed of themselves. "The confessional is solely for the sacrament of penance," he says; "Something which undoubtedly you both need badly." Several days later, we read in the paper that there was an earthquake in Assisi. We have a pang of guilt, justified or not.

After lunch, we are back on the *Autostrada,* from where we exit at Deruta, a small town in the middle of Umbria, famous for its hand painted ceramics. Here, in the afterglow of too much wine—we buy beautiful tableware and tiles as well as a 47-inch round "garden table" with an iron base weighing close to two hundred pounds that we nevertheless ship home to Florida.

After a stop at the ancient monastery, La Badia di Orvieto, Enrico drops us off at our hotel, on the outskirts of Siena—he is practically in tears to see us go. Embracing Bill with a burly hug, he tells us we are his favorite Americans. We assure him we will return.

Bill sets up his portable easel by the window of our hotel room and begins to capture the panoramic views. Several days later, we hire a driver to take us to Florence; now, in addition to our overabundance of luggage, we are dragging along wet canvases and an easel. I will always remember entering the city over the Ponte alla Vittoria and seeing the Arno River for the first time—marveling at the sheer beauty of this Renaissance city. I could not have imagined then that we would end up living and working there for all these years.

They Love Me in Italy

As soon as Bill started to paint in Siena, he evolved from tourist to artist and stopped shaving. We were officially cool as we arrived in the most famous art city in the world—and looking the part.

Our heads still filled with the marvels of Rome, we were disappointed in our Florence hotel on the outskirts of the city. I remembered a friend telling us of a tiny hotel in the city center and we moved to the Hermitage, on the top floor of a medieval building by the Ponte Vecchio. We spend two days sightseeing, visiting among other sights the Duomo, the Uffizi Gallery, and the Galleria dell' Accademia to see the real "David" by Michelangelo. We walked everywhere and followed our *Eyewitness Travel Guide* diligently.

Then, giving ourselves a break from nonstop sightseeing, we rented a car and headed for Montecatini Terme where I had booked the five-star Grand Hotel & La Pace, a surprising bargain. It was luxurious, with massively wide hallways lined with framed black and white photos of the famous people who have been guests here; Prince Rainier of Monaco and Grace Kelly, Audrey Hepburn, Spencer Tracy, Orson Welles.

The town has numerous spas and beautiful architecture, the most splendid being the neo-classical Terme Tettuccio, the oldest and most famous. There we bought a ticket and were given a glass mug for the healing (salty tasting) waters, which we drank while listening to orchestral music. Music is part of the process, as is eating lightly while you're getting your body in balance. The idea is to ingest the right amount of mineral-laden water in an environment that's relaxing and conducive to healing. Amidst the magnificent buildings, fountains, and beautifully landscaped gardens are numerous stone buildings housing toilets. After several days of taking the "the cure," Bill decided he was healed and opted to take the funicular railway up to the ancient village of Montecatini Alto to paint.

Montecatini Terme is known for its thermal mud baths, which are said to cure every ailment. This treatment worked well until the second day. While sitting naked in a tub, covered in the dark hot sludge, I find what appears to be a large toenail. I call for someone who can speak English and ask if the dirt is recycled. "Yes, of course, Madam." The news that "my" mud wasn't just mine marked the dramatic end of my treatments.

We left for Pisa, without regret, where we set up a base for several side trips. We drove to Portofino, only to discover that there is one road in. It was Sunday, and police had set up a roadblock, and were turning people away, as the town has reached its limit for tourists and parking places. But I had not come this far to be turned away. I remembered the name of the most famous hotel. I opened the phrase book, got out of the car, and walked to the policeman. Smiling broadly, I say, *"Ciao, andiamo all'Hotel Splendido." "OK, vai avanti,"* he says, waving to Bill, whose head is sticking out of the driver's window, wondering what I am doing. And that is how we got to spend a glorious day in Portofino.

With his beard growing fuller by the day, Bill carries his collapsible French easel everywhere and happily paints our travels. Life is good—until we arrive at the Florence train station, with four massive suitcases, the easel, and three wet paintings. A man offers to help us get on the train, carrying our bags and pushing us from the rear. Finally, settled in our seats, across the table from one another, Bill says, "Do you have my wallet?" This black wallet and a black comb are never far from his right rear pocket, but now they are in someone else's pocket. Travel lesson number one: Never take a trip by train with wet canvases and too much luggage. And *never* accept the kindness of strangers who could be gypsy pick-pockets.

When we arrive in Venice—or La Serenissima, which is what the Italians call that not-so-serene but most magical city in Italy -- we fall in love. Mercifully, there is an American Express office, and they are able to get us a replacement credit card by noon the following day.

—⊗⊗⊗—

Bill and I knew each other only six months when we married, each for the second time. We were in our early forties--both of us long divorced, me seventeen years, he fourteen, each with two children, all four in college, when we were introduced in Boston by mutual friends. It was instant attraction. Now after eight years, we were somewhere between making love three times a day and adjusting to shared finances and each other's children. In 1997, with no cell phones or email, we were free and exploring together; as though we were at the beginning of our romance. We had never known such complete bliss. We were perfect traveling companions. A plan started to germinate in both of our heads.

Following our return to the States and our life in Florida, Bill paints long, furious hours—as many as three or four canvases at a time, using sketches he drew on our trip. He is capturing the landscapes and colors of Italy. He paints in his studio as well as outside on the beach where we live, wearing a straw hat and a sarong. The Gulf view gives him inspiration, he says, and he likes to paint outside.

Bill will now only drink Italian wine and he insists on throwing around his few Italian phrases, answering the phone, *"Ciao,"* or *"Pronto."*

Although he has his own small studio/gallery on First Street, in Sarasota, the Ziegenfuss Gallery on Palm Avenue wants a show in April featuring his new Italian paintings. *They Love Me in Italy* sells out. He is featured in local newspaper articles, which say he is "serving up art and life—with gusto." "Kelley is the only one of us who paints his life," one writer says. "He could well be one of the great artists of his time," says another.

Buoyed by this success, we start discussing the possibility of living in Italy, maybe for a semester. Although Bill attended post-graduate classes at the School of the Museum of Fine Arts in Boston, which was a turning point for him, he begins to talk of studying in Italy. I sense another turning point on the horizon. Our ninth anniversary arrives in June, and we put our beautiful Gulf-front property up for sale.

Although Bill painted and sketched all his life, business and family needs intervened, and he earned his money elsewhere. Now he wants to paint full time. As the months pass, the beard grows— and the dream starts to take on a life of its own. Bill begins to research art schools offering graduate degrees in painting—in Rome, Florence and Venice.

Just Do It

I n September 1998 we return to Rome, Venice, and Florence to look for a place to live. Enrico, our driver from the previous year, meets us, this time wearing a suit. He is thrilled to see his good friends. He takes us around Rome, so Bill can check out some of the art schools. We consider living in the city; it is beautiful, but the country's largest and most populated *commune*—too grand for us. Enrico tells us, "If you really want to live in Italy, you're probably better off in Florence." He explains that it is a more livable city than Rome, comparing it to Boston, a city we know well and love. Florence is a university town as well as the center for Renaissance art, and the most centrally located of all three cities.

We cross Rome off our list, and set off for Venice. We decide to stay in Padua for a week and take the train to Venice every day. The entire time, the city is flooded; we wear boots and walk on wooden planks in Piazza San Marco, the principal public square of Venice. Bill does not care for the school there, as it is more concerned with printmaking than painting. They ask him if he would like to come and teach, but he politely declines.

We arrive in Florence and decide that because it is a small, walking city—almost a provincial town—and ground zero for Western art, that it is the best place for us. Bill applies to Lorenzo de' Medici Institute to pursue a Master's degree in painting.

"This is the home of Leonardo and Michelangelo," he says. "It's the most serious city in the world to study painting—it is a living museum." Our plan is in place: he will study art history and painting the following fall. And me? I convince myself that as a writer, I can write anywhere.

I remember when as a young divorcee and mother of two, in my 20s I fantasized about moving to Florence and putting my children in the American International School, which I had read about. But I did not have anywhere near the finances needed for such a move; living in Florence remained a fantasy I cherished. Now I have the opportunity.

We leave for Italy September 1, for the fall semester, with a plan to stay until Christmas. Bill will attend school and concentrate on painting. I will study Italian, write my magnum opus, and take cooking classes. We are in our mid-50s, our children are

grown, college graduates, and gainfully employed—
so why not? Or, as they say in Italy, *"Perche no?"*
We will be the poster couple for AARP. Instead of
dreaming the dream, we will *live* the dream.

Our new home

In August 1999, we arrive at the apartment on Lungarno Archibusieri No. 6 that we have made arrangements to rent through student housing—sight unseen. Bill had explained that we were a bit older than the usual student, and then lied, "We're not twenty; we're in our forties."

The apartment, in what we learn is a Renaissance palazzo, is beautiful but far too big and very old. It could sleep 12 students—and has. Living in Sarasota, where anything built before 1950 is considered antique, the contrast is shocking. In Florence, a few hundred years old is borderline contemporary.

I pass through the entrance hall and there are two massive rooms on either side, with 25-foot ceilings. The owner, Maria, shows us the largest bedroom and bathroom. A sign in English hangs on the wall next to the water heater: "Turn switch off after using shower or it may blow up." There is an alcove with a consecrated chapel and votive candles and a statue of the Madonna and a kneeling bench for prayer. Three concrete steps lead to the windowsill, where we can look out and see people walking in the Vasari Corridor, a private elevated walkway running parallel to our apartment, linking the Palazzo Vecchio to the Palazzo Pitti. This was built so that members of the Medici family—in particular, Catherine de Medici, the wife of Cosimo—could move between residences without having to step onto the street below and mix with the common people. It is now open for guided tours only. All of this the owner relates in limited English.

Our landlady recommends a nearby restaurant, Buca dell'Orafo, but after circling the area too many times and not being able to find it, we arrive at Buca Poldo, also around the corner from where we live. One of the first people we meet is a waiter named Yaseen, a young man who is from Casablanca, and speaks both fluent Italian and English. He explains the wine and food and introduces us to the owner, Franco.

The trattoria becomes our second home, where we come for dinner twice a week in the years that follow. It is also where Bill comes nightly during my absences from Florence. In the warm months, we sit outside under umbrellas in the small alley at Chiasso degli Armagnati, directly off Piazza della Signoria. *Buca* translates as "hole, but is slang for basement. Many restaurants start with the word, which basically means you must go down one or two flights of stairs to access the restaurant. This is where we will go in the winter months, when it is too cold to sit outside.

Yaseen is instrumental in telling us where to get what we need—like a king-size mattress to put over the top of two twin beds in the master bedroom. Today, we could go to IKEA but it was not there at the time. He tells us which is the best Italian language school—Dante Aligheri—and about a food market, Pegna, that will deliver.

His favorite song is "American Woman," by the "Guess Who." He is always singing the same verse:

American woman, stay away from me
American woman, mama, let me be

Yaseen is an invaluable friend and source of Florentine information until he is deported a few years later—allegedly for committing lewd and lascivious acts with a young American student. What can that possibly mean in Italy? We are shocked, but admittedly intrigued.

Tests

Bill enrolls in the Lorenzo de' Medici School, where he was supposed to be in the conceptual painting program, but he finds out there's a test. It turns out that there is only room for twelve students and seventeen have been accepted. Five must be eliminated. He does well enough on the test that he is admitted and begins his semester. He is busy at school, painting every day. Meanwhile, I am dealing with conflicting life events, which include finishing my newest book about second marriages, planning the imminent wedding of my daughter in New York, and awaiting the birth of my son's baby, my first grandchild. Our house in Sarasota is for sale. We were into year 10 of our marriage when we embarked on our adventure, and we were each still trying to assert our individuality. There were the classic ingredients for marital conflict in our clashing priorities. It is a battle of the sexes, colliding with the innate complexities of family. We needed to find out how to be a couple together. Our time in Europe couldn't be about me following his dream or his following mine at the expense of our individual dreams. I had to figure out how to find my place.

Most of the arrangements are in place for the wedding while we are settling into daily life in Florence, but my head is still planning the menu and choosing flowers. My daughter, a student at Columbia University Medical School in New York, has little time to be involved. Planning a wedding for 150 people from across the ocean, particularly one in Manhattan poses many a challenge. I don't have my mother-of-the bride outfit. I flash back to when my son got married and his future mother-in-law announced to me after describing her "party dress" that she was, after all, the "second most important person at the wedding."

I begin the search for my wedding attire. I look all over Florence, in shop after shop, for a dress or suit and find nothing that fits. This is the first time I notice the body types of the Florentine women. They are thin and fit. They walk or ride their bicycles, they don't eat pasta, *and* most of them smoke. This leaves them with firm, thin thighs, and they all seem to have gorgeous cleavage. I have the opposite body type. Every outfit I try on is too big on the top and too small on the bottom. And at size 6, I'm not even a big or overweight person by American standards.

I begin to realize that Florentine women wear their clothes skin tight. If it buttons or zips, it's your size—forget about comfort or breathing. I will have to find something in the States when I fly back two weeks before the event. Bill does not understand the extent of my responsibilities as event planner for this important occasion. It is not possible to please *everyone* or be *every* place. I leave Bill in Florence, where he is having way too much fun with the younger-than-our- children students at his school, and return to Florida. As the John Lennon lyrics go, "Life is what happens when you're busy making other plans." Bill joins me in New York in time for the wedding.

Spousal Credits

We take a call on the glorious September day of my daughter's wedding as we stand on the roof-deck of the Bryant Park Grill, posing for family photos.

"It's a cash offer, there's a thirty-day close, with no contingencies," the broker says. We had put our Sarasota home on the market fifteen months before and now we are accepting this life-altering offer, on a Manhattan rooftop. The anticipated sale of our home added to the feelings of new beginnings on this happiest of days.

Bill returns to school a few days after the wedding, flying back to Florence alone. My daughter and her new husband go off on their honeymoon, and I return to Florida to organize the move, and await the birth of my grandchild, who will be born to my son and his then-wife eight days later in Boston.

After the birth, I fly to Boston, help my son, daughter-in-law, and the new baby settle in, buy what they need, and then return to Florida to pack up Bill's and my life by myself—10 years of *stuff*. As compensation, I insist that when I return to Italy, we go to Positano for a week of rest and romance and stay at the five-star San Pietro Hotel. I am cashing in what I refer to as "spousal credits"—lots of them. Positano and this storied hotel is a place I have always wanted to go. Of course, my darling husband has to agree.

The hotel lives up to its reputation, its elegant rooms overlooking the Mediterranean from a clifftop perch. One evening, following a delectable lobster dinner at Cambusa, an old fishing shack-turned-seafood-restaurant on the beach, several miles from the San Pietro, Bill suggests we walk back to the hotel and explore the town on the way. But hours pass as we trudge up and down the steep and winding streets. Now it is two in the morning and although Bill won't admit it, we are lost.

"I know this city like the back of my hand," he assures me.

My high-heeled, sandaled feet are swollen and throbbing. "That's it, call a cab. I am not taking one more step," I say. As if by magic, just then we spot a sign stuck to a tree: "Taxi Mimi." Bill fishes in his pocket for some coins, puts them in the slot of a pay phone nearby, and dials the number. A woman answers. He explains in his best Italian where we are, and the woman says, "Mimi coming."

Ten minutes pass and a gentleman around the age of 60 drives up in a black Mercedes sedan, dressed in dark slacks, starched white shirt, and navy tie. I've never been so happy to see anyone in my life. He drives us back to the hotel and asks if we have been to Mount Vesuvius and Pompeii. We have not, so he hands us his card and says he will pick us up at nine the following morning. "What are the chances of this guy actually showing up tomorrow morning?" Bill asks, before answering the question himself. "Slim to none." We undress and drop into bed, exhausted.

Domenico (Mimi) shows up precisely at 9 a.m. in the morning. It is a searingly hot day as we drive to Pompeii. On the way, Mimi asks whom we know in Florence and if we know his best friend, Lisa Peruggi. When we say no, he calls her and passes the phone to us in the back seat. Bill speaks with her and in no time discovers she is originally from Hingham, Massachusetts, where two of our grown children now live. He says she is funny and sounds like Auntie Mame. She says to call her when we return to Florence.

Lisa

Back in Florence, I begin asking around about where I might take cooking lessons. Bill's teacher gives me the name of Faith Willinger, the American cookbook author and authority on Italian food, who lives in Florence. I call and leave her a message. When she returns the call, she tells me her cooking classes are $400 for half a day, but they are over for the season.

Then I call Lisa to introduce myself and enlist her help. She says that Faith Willinger's price is "perfectly ridiculous" and insists on giving me a cooking lesson herself. Lisa, I will come learn, is very generous, but she is a Yankee and would not squander $400 on a half-day cooking class. A few days later, I meet her for the first time and to learn how to cook like the locals.

Lisa's home is a contemporary, architecturally pleasing residence in Piazza del Carmine, one of the main squares of the Oltrarno district of Florence, dominated by the majestic Church of Santa Maria del Carmine, with its landmark frescoes by the early Renaissance master Masaccio, just steps from her house. At the other end of the square lies her preferred local eatery, Trattoria del Carmine, which serves an authentic, typically Florentine menu at reasonable prices.

Her apartment, a remodeled 14th century cloister, with a first-floor entrance and a long living room leading to an outdoor garden, is perfect for entertaining. The kitchen and the formal dining room are side by side, the dining room walls lined with magnificent tapestries, a gift from her "Grandmamma," she informs me.

When I arrive, Lisa has all the ingredients we will need grouped by recipe, next to large, well-worn stainless steel pots. We drink some wine and make vegetable soup and a ragu sauce and a delectable veal stew. "Now, you go home, I'll have a little nap, and you'll come back for dinner at 8 with your husband." This, I learn, is Lisa's daily routine: lunch with a little wine, a nap, then dinner with lots of wine.

Sometimes when you talk to someone prior to meeting him or her, they turn out to be nothing like what you imagine. This is not the case with my new friend. She reminds me on the phone of Julia Child, with her deep voice and patrician New England accent. When we meet, she is exactly the person I had envisioned from talking with her. Opinionated, witty, and warm, she is, as Bill said, the Auntie Mame we all wish we had had growing up. With nothing more than an introduction from Mimi, the driver, she has purchased all the ingredients for a cooking lesson, which she gives me as a gift.

"My first husband's mother taught me to cook," she sings out in Julia fashion, as we are getting started. "One thing or another." This is her signature expression, which she uses to end many a stream-of-consciousness thought—often when she doesn't feel like talking any more.

At 62 years old, she is a stately woman, tall, with auburn hair that she wears in a neat ponytail. Smart and full of fun, she arrived in Florence in the mid-1950s when she was 18 years old, married an Italian doctor a couple of years later, had three children with him, and became one of the fixtures of Florentine society. But he cheated, in typical Italian fashion, and she found out. "There's an old Italian saying," Lisa tells me, "*Occhio non vede, cuore non duole* (if the eye doesn't see, the heart doesn't suffer). I saw."

Divorce and separation were against the law in Italy at that time. After 19 years of marriage, at the age of 37, she and four women in her bridge club— three whose husbands had mistresses—flew to Haiti and got divorces. Five years later, she married her current husband, the extremely gorgeous Florentine architect and "impassioned" Communist, Marcello. In between husbands, there was an affair with an Italian actor she met in Positano at the home of Franco Zeffirelli.

That evening, Bill and I arrive for dinner with several bottles of wine. Only after all the guests are gathered does Marcello make his grand entrance.

The French doors from the bedroom open, and out he steps, dressed in mahogany-colored slacks, a fitted white shirt, and paisley ascot, with a camel-hair sports jacket draped over his shoulders, sleeves dangling at his sides. He is a stunning man in his late 60s, athletically built with a shock of thick, wavy, white hair. He smiles seductively and murmurs, *"Buonasera,"* taking both of my hands in his as he kisses each side of my face. He then descends the three steps to the dining room and takes his seat at the head of the table. His chair is an antique, upholstered throne that looks like it was custom made for a Pope, or at least a cardinal.

Bill is required to study Italian at his art school and is somewhat conversant. He makes every effort to speak Italian, because Marcello refuses to speak English, despite the fact that he is married to an American. Lisa talks about him in the third person, referring to him as "hubby," but we're sure he understands everything.

"We've been married for over 20 years and he's spent a lot of time in the States," Lisa says. "But he makes absolutely no attempt to speak English." She pauses, then adds, "He's a Communist, you know." We come to find out that he is a Communist, who travels only business class and drives a Porsche.

The Maestro

With Bill back in school, I finally settle into a routine and start writing. Married to the "Maestro," as he is called here, I have to find strategies to remain busy while my exuberantly extroverted painter spouse is gone all day. Except for Lisa, I know no Americans. Our friends in Florence consist of a diverse group of kids from Scuola Lorenzo de' Medici, along with Rose and Claire, Bill's South African art teachers, a Lesbian couple slightly younger than we are, whom we adore. Claire is an elegant former ballerina and Rose is her masculine counterpart. Besides being great educators, they are wonderfully witty and wise, full of information and interested in everything.

For our first Thanksgiving in Florence, I want the traditional dinner of turkey, squash, mashed potatoes, and gravy. We walk to Harry's American Bar, located along the river at Via Lungarno Amerigo Vespucci, which advertises a "full American turkey dinner." We have no reservation, and after several glasses of wine at the bar and no promise of seating, we leave and go to Buca Mario, where we have a "full Tuscan dinner" instead. I'm feeling far from home, and vow to plan ahead next year.

By December we were coming to the end of our first taste of Florentine living. Our relationship with Florence unfolded like a typical love affair. First came the romance of living in a foreign country—we were newly in love and everything was perfect. Next came the honeymoon, the experimentation. We were happy to cocoon in our private hideout. We knew few people, but who needed the rest of the world?

We settled into everyday life, making an effort to keep it simple. We had no car, so we walked everywhere. On weekends we took the train to Rome or rented a car for a leisurely getaway in Chianti. By the time the honeymoon had ended, we knew the foibles and faults of our beloved. We were living in a country whose language neither of us could speak, despite Bill's language lessons at his school. It was difficult to get serious things done. Sure, we could buy a cappuccino, but trying to get an airline flight changed was an impossible challenge. Like newlyweds who leave the cap off the toothpaste, we discovered petty annoyances.

Not having the luxury of a clothes dryer at first seems charming. I hang the laundry on a wooden clothes rack and it dries overnight. Bill's socks become stiff loofahs, as do the towels. Then there are the mosquitoes; our apartment on the Arno has no screens on the massive windows. And there is the ever-present dog poop on the streets that we have to play hopscotch to avoid.

But eventually, we arrive at the total acceptance and joy of embracing another culture and its people. How can we not love the friendly people, the food, the Tuscan wine, the history and culture that are everywhere around us? I start taking language lessons, too, and we learn to do things the Italian way. We find Luca the butcher at *Sant'Ambrogio* market, and Carlo the dry cleaner. In no time I can at least buy groceries. I converse in my own version of tourist Italian—all with a big smile and a sincere effort, all one tense.

—⚬⚬⚬—

Saying a fond "Ciao, Firenze," we return to our newly rented condo in Sarasota and become accustomed to our temporary quarters with no big house to look after. The following summer, in June 2000, Bill has his first one-man art show at the Walter Wickiser Gallery in New York's Soho, featuring many of his Italian paintings. We are happy to learn that our Florentine friend, Lisa Peruggi, has an apartment in the city, and she happens to be in town during Bill's show. Ever the generous hostess, she insists on having a dinner party for us to introduce us to her friends, which is how we meet Rosaria and

Ferdinando Frescobaldi of the 700-year-old wine family, one of the oldest and most distinguished in Florence. They will become friends who remain central to our lives in Florence.

The gallery sells all the Italian paintings from Tuscany, Positano, Tivoli, and Portofino. Bill, thrilled with the result of the show, wants to return to Florence; I had thought we were done. Lisa, who knows our Florence apartment is not really suitable, invites us for coffee the next morning. She calls her friend Suzanne Pitcher, a real estate agent in Florence and hands Bill the phone. Suzanne assures Bill that she can provide much better accommodations for us. We can look forward to continuing our adventure for at least another year.

My fourth book, *The Second Time Around,* is released by William Morrow. Our good friend, Brian Johnson, lead singer for AC/DC, is on tour and is performing in New York. We go to his concert. It is a joyous time for us with Bill's successful art show and my new book. It was our modern day version of *A Movable Feast.*

And so we rent another apartment, sight unseen, through our new friend Suzanne, who is from Australia. She came to Florence in November 1966 after the Arno River flooded, damaging or destroying millions of masterpieces of art and rare books. It was the worst flood in the city since 1557. People came from all over the world, like Suzanne, to help rescue, preserve and restore the works of art. They were known as "mud angels"—*angeli del fango*. Suzanne stayed and married a Florentine and together they had one son, Corso. Then she got divorced and joined the real estate business of sales and rentals.

Different Priorities

September 2000: Challenges begin to cloud our bliss. I have a contractual obligation for a book tour. After much discussion, we reach a compromise—of sorts. Bill agrees to delay his semester at school two weeks and stay for the beginning of my local book appearances. Then off he goes, back to Florence, and I go on the road promoting my most recent relationship tome.

Having three books published on this subject has made me an *authority*. The irony of the situation is that my husband is alone in Florence, painting nude models, while I am appearing on TV—doling out advice on how one can achieve the optimal level of marital bliss, "everything you need to know to make your remarriage happy," as per the subtitle.

I appear on numerous TV shows, including *Oprah*, as a "relationship expert." I freely quote Zsa Zsa Gabor's line, "Men are like fires; they go out when unattended." But I am not heeding my own advice. If I want to stay a married "relationship expert," I knew I had better join Bill in Italy.

My father had not been feeling well for a few months. The day before I planned to return, my mother called to tell me he had inoperable cancer. I cry all the way as I drive to my parents' house 20 minutes away from mine in Sarasota. I kiss my father hello, and in his usual dignified way, he says, "Death and taxes, we all have to die. I've had a good life."

I visit with him and he looks okay—the same. We have a glass of wine together and he encourages me to be with my husband. I have no idea how much time he has left and reluctantly leave as he assures me we can be in touch by phone. I am now a woman torn between two men—my terminally ill father and my extroverted artist-husband—and two worlds, an ocean apart: Florida and Florence.

After a separation of one month, with bags packed, I head back to Florence. Bill greets me at Fiumicino Airport in Rome at 9 a.m. with a big smile, a hard kiss, and his strong, protective embrace. He got up at dawn and has travelled three hours to pick me up in a Mercedes van with his new *best* friend, David Tweed, who is a professional tour guide and driver. David is originally from London and speaks Italian with a Cockney accent.

I see the new apartment for the first time. Suzanne has found us a cheerful and colorfully furnished place to live. The building directly overlooks the Arno River in the Oltrarno area. It is quiet and more modern than last year's massive rooms filled with dark, uncomfortable antique furniture across the Arno. The building has an elevator *and* a doorman. I look out the window and see the Uffizi Gallery, directly opposite on the other side of the river. This residence, at 33 Lungarno Torrigiani is on the fifth floor—130 stairs. I will try to walk the stairs once a day, I promise myself—the Italian Stairmaster.

There is an entrance hall, a bright kitchen with dishwasher and washing machine (but no dryer, in the Italian manner), two bedrooms, and two bathrooms. The windows in the spacious living room open to the Arno, and the study, with a pullout couch, has the same magnificent view. Bill has set up a temporary painting studio in this room, his easel facing the window. He has hired a weekly cleaning person. "She whistles show tunes and doesn't do windows," he tells me.

The doorman, Renzo, sits in a wood and glass enclosed cubicle on the ground floor of the entrance to the building in a cloud of blue cigarette smoke— when he is there, which is not often. He walks to the local bar for coffee or a drink about 10 times a day and hangs up a sign in his absence: *"Torno subito."* Although we know it means, "I return immediately," we learn how elastic the word "subito" can be.

What I come to love especially about living in Florence, besides the obvious beauty, history, and culture, is the anonymity. There are no social expectations except when our friend Lisa provided invitations, and that always guaranteed fun—a diverse assemblage of Florentines and Americans with a few Australians thrown in, for even more liveliness.

After admiring the apartment, Bill and I stroll across the Ponte Vecchio, lined on both sides with jewelry shops, go to our favorite hangout, Caffé Rivoire, in Piazza della Signoria, order cheese omelets for lunch, and despite a damp chill in the air decide it is not too cold to sit outside. We never tire of the view of the spouting Neptune Fountain and the Palazzo Vecchio, surely the most beautiful town hall in the world. As always, we choose the table in the front so we can be in Salvatore's section.

Bill has favorite waiters all over Florence, and Salvatore is one of them. They call him "Maestro" and bow when he enters. *"Ciao, come stai?"* And to me, *"Sempre bella,"* and *"Troppo elegante."*

"This is the most serious city in the world to study painting," Bill says. Artists are treated with great respect in Italy. "They fucking love me here, I am the quintessential Renaissance man."

An accordion player comes to the entrance. He is dressed in a black trench coat. He plays "Arrivederci, Roma," but changes the lyrics to *"Arrivederci, Florence,"* then switches to "Somewhere Over the Rainbow." His companion passes around a hat, asking for money. It's so corny and touristy, but I have a little lump in my throat. I think about how happy I am to be here.

After lunch, we return home for a nap. I awaken to the musical sound of bells ringing throughout the city. They ring alone or in unison for many reasons—to chime in the hours of the day, to celebrate a wedding, to call worshippers to Mass. "Don't open your eyes yet," Bill says. I hear him unfasten the old, creaky, wooden bedroom shutters. "Okay," he says. "Take a look at the Palazzo Vecchio tower and the Campanile from your bedroom window."

I get up and go to the window. Leaning out, I can see all the way to Santa Croce. I poke my head further out into the noisy day, with motorbikes speeding by in the street beneath me, and I look left to see the Ponte Vecchio. I turn to view Bill, posing in the nude, impersonating Michelangelo's *David*. "Your choice, David or me?"

<hr />

I am having trouble sleeping at night; I am plagued with nightmares, concerned about my father. Bill says he will read to me. He decides on *Hannibal*, the Thomas Harris sequel to *Silence of the Lambs*. He's already read it and told me not to, because it's too scary for me, but he wants to read the part that takes place in Florence, because he thinks this will steer my mind in a new direction. I might still have bad dreams, but they will be *different* nightmares.

Oddly, I sleep better than I have in weeks.

The next morning, Bill is like a little kid as he spreads out the map of Florence on the living room table and traces the path of Dr. Fell (Hannibal Lecter) and Ronaldo Pazzi that he read about last night. We realize that in the book, Lecter lives on Via de' Bardi. This street runs along the back of the apartment building where we are living. So this fictitious character lives three doors away from us, travels the same path we do, and goes to the same shops and restaurants. We decide to explore and see if the name on the door of his building—Palazzo Capponi—is real or fictitious. We discover to our delight that the name on the building is, indeed, Palazzo Capponi. Bill now wants to climb the steep hill to Forte di Belvedere. I want to have a cappuccino. We do both.

We have no hot water again and I'm getting frustrated. Today two men came to fix it, and it *was* working. One hour later I go to take a shower, and it is ice.

"Life is not a five star hotel," Bill says in response to my griping. Three workmen arrive with a ladder to change one light bulb in the hallway ceiling. "How many Italians does it take to change a light bulb?"

Bill asks. He is so content to be here, to be living his dream, to be painting every day, he doesn't care if anything works.

I sign up for language and cooking classes at Centro Ponte Vecchio in Piazza del Mercato Nuovo. We go to the Mercado Centrale, Central Market to learn some shopping and food vocabulary. Mariangela, our teacher, has given us a photocopy of foods to ask for at the market, as well as a list of appropriate phrases we might need. Our assignment is to buy things, or at least to find out how much items cost, and to converse with the shopkeepers. The Mercado Centrale is a massive indoor food market. The first floor is mainly butchers and fishmongers and stalls selling cheeses and olive oil. The upstairs is wall-to-wall vegetables and fruit stands.

After shopping, we go to the kitchen at the language school. The class consists of me, six non-English-speaking Japanese students roughly age 20—though most of the Japanese here do speak English very well—and one guy of 28 with hair sprayed or dyed canary yellow, also from Japan. "Me no gay boy," he says, and the girls giggle.

We stand in our white aprons around a small table, taking turns mixing and chopping. The menu consists of pasta with clams, mussels, and calamari. We cook for two hours, and the girls are conscientious, wanting to do everything; mix the eggs, stir the contents of the frying pan, and cut the vegetables. They do all of this with great precision. When making the dessert, I learn that tiramisu consists of raw eggs and mascarpone cheese, which is 70% fat. I make a mental note not to order it in the future. To my further dismay, I discover I remember very little Italian from the past year.

When the meal is ready at 1 p.m., it is served on the outside terrace of the school. The moment the food is presented, the students from the language school descend on the table, loading their plastic plates with the food. I find this puzzling, since they haven't paid for the food or the cooking lesson.

My father's condition has stabilized, so we make plans to go to Sicily during Bill's semester break from school at the end of October. I book plane reservations and am successful in getting accommodations at the Hotel San Domenico Palace in Taormina for three days. Then we will drive to Palermo and spend one night at the Villa Igiea Grand Hotel before returning to Florence.

The good thing about traveling around Italy this late in the season is that there are fewer tourists, so there's a greater possibility of reserving the best hotels, and the rates are lower. I give my brothers and my mother the phone numbers where I will be in case my father's condition changes.

We arrive by taxi at the airport in Florence for our 7 a.m. flight to Sicily, only to find it has been cancelled because of fog. The ticket agent, with no apologies, says they will try to put us on a bus to Bologna for a 10 a.m. flight. Bill is grouchy and says he's not going. We get a cappuccino at the airport coffee shop and Bill decides he does want to go, despite the inconvenience.

The bus speeds along the slick highway in the drizzle and smog, and an hour and a half later passes the Bologna exit. An older man, whose wife is yelling at him, goes to the front of the bus and is shouting in Italian, demanding to know why we did not exit at Bologna. He starts yanking the driver's jacket. The driver is now half standing, his left hand on the steering wheel while defending himself against the attacker with his right arm. Everyone starts yelling for the guy to sit down, because we are all terrified of an accident.

No announcement is made, but we eventually pause at a rest stop. Through our limited Italian and another passenger's equally limited English, we find out that Bologna is also fogged in, so we are being redirected to the Venice airport.

"So basically we are practically going to Switzerland in order to fly to Italy's southernmost point," Bill says. "Infuckingcredible!"

We finally leave Venice at 12:45 p.m., wearied. It is raining lightly when we land in Sicily. We rent a car at Catania-Fontanarossa Airport; it takes us 45 minutes to drive to the Hotel San Domenico Palace in Taormina, a luxury hotel in a former Dominican monastery with superb furnishings and gardens. We decide it was all worth the insanity of the trip just to be here. Although it is still sprinkling, we want to explore the town. We find a place to have a sandwich and a glass of wine; then we walk to the Greek theatre perched at the edge of the Mediterranean, but it has closed for the day.

We take a nap before dinner in the massive antique bed with pressed white linen sheets. I have booked one of the best rooms and wonder if the abbot lived in this huge space.

The early evening mist has turned to a torrential downpour, so we opt for a 9 p.m. dinner in the hotel dining room. I feel I should go back to the room and phone my mother. I eventually get through to her and she tells me the bad news that my father has been given two weeks to live. Now we have to figure out how to get out of here. Bill attempts to comfort me by retelling the story about how his father was given two weeks to live in January, slipped into a coma, woke up singing Irish songs on St. Patrick's Day in March, and didn't die till April 5.

It is not easy getting a flight out of the Catania Airport, especially since our tickets are from Falcone-Borsellino Airport in Palermo later in the week, but somehow, American Express pulls it off and we fly to Pisa, from where a taxi driver takes us to Florence.

The driver's phone rings continually. It is programmed with a special ring—songs from his computer. Did it himself, he says, in reasonably good English that he learned from listening to American music, he tells us. The phone's sound is Tchaikovsky's

"Dance of the Sugar Plum Fairies." That's the fall tune. He explains to Bill that during the summer it was Bob Marley's "Redemption" and in the spring, John Lennon's "Give Peace a Chance."

Bill says, "Okay, phase one complete." Now we have to get to Florida. Getting out of Sicily was the most difficult. As soon as we get back to the apartment, we get out the credit card and call American Express. "Phase two," Bill announces energetically. He has a mission.

I get Cathy in Miami, who is very sympathetic when I explain the circumstances and our need for an immediate flight to Florida. I'm hoping our last remaining phone card won't run out and disconnect us. We're all set to leave Florence at 6:30 a.m. with David the English driver once again, heading to Pisa. We are booked on British Air, from Pisa to Gatwick in England with a three-hour layover, and then nonstop to Tampa. Cathy kindly upgrades us to first class.

"Phase two complete," Bill says. We decide to go pick up the email confirmation of our prepaid tickets at the Internet café (there is no WiFi in our apartment) and get a pizza for dinner. We head to Golden View Open Bar on Via de Bardi, which, Bill tells me, is this year's new restaurant discovery.

The alarm goes off at 6 A.M. My eyelids and under-eyes are puffed-up, leaving slits to peer through. I shower quickly and apply ice cubes to reduce the swelling.

David Tweed arrives punctually at 6:30. We drive in the darkness, on slippery streets through mist and a light rain, back to Pisa airport. We take off on schedule for London. Bill smiles at me and extends his hand to be shaken. "Phase three," he says. We are leaving Italy. This will be 33 hours of travel since departing Sicily until we get home, he tells me.

We depart London after a two hour delay. The flight attendant brings us glasses of crisp white wine, along with warm nuts in a white ceramic dish. Bill clinks his glass to mine. "To Bud," he says. "This one's for you, Dad," I say, hoping we make it on time to say goodbye.

My father makes it through the week—Bill calls him "Bionic Bud." We sit in the hospital room, Mother doing her crossword puzzle. He naps, but she ignores this.

"Bud, give me the name of a Zola book that starts with N," she demands.

He opens his eyes. "Emile Zola."

She must think that if she keeps him talking, he will not die. "Come on, now, a Zola book, four letters, starting with N."

"Nana," he says.

She talks incessantly over the unrelenting hum of the machinery. Dad lies with his eyes closed, colorless, oxygen tube in his nose; the constant beep, beep,

beep from the medical equipment keeping him awake. The process of dying is not serene. Occasionally he removes the apparatus, pushes it up, and rests it on his forehead. A green bottle is suspended overhead to the right of the bed. It adds water to the oxygen to help prevent nosebleeds, the nurse tells me.

"I need the name of a Kenny Rogers song, four letters, starting with L."

"Lady," he says without opening his eyes.

I sit watching Dad. He's reaching his hands out again. He seems worried in his dream. I gaze at the two hanging bags on the left side of his bed. I am unable to leave the hospital. We sit. Mother does not stop talking; every now and then I tune in. Bill attempts to interrupt her by changing the subject, but instead of answering him, she continues her Molly Bloom soliloquy.

"County Monahan," she is saying. "That's where my mother's family is from. My mother's father, Thomas, was an accountant, and he worked for Candy & Smith Brick Company—Twenty-seventh Street, New York. He graduated from Trinity College in Dublin. He used to bring people over from Ireland and set them up with jobs.

"Catherine Marie, born in County Monahan," she says to me. "That's who you are named for." My middle name is Marie.

My daughter the doctor, who has married a Jewish doctor and now is proficient in making

Matzo ball soup, tells me that being at the hospital all day is like sitting Shiva before someone has died.

A young woman breezes into the room, wearing a starched white hospital coat. "I'm from the psychology department," she says. "I'm here for an evaluation."

"Of what?" I ask.

"Is the patient suffering from depression?"

"Wouldn't you be if you were dying?"

Bill has decided to return to school in Italy on Monday. He reiterates that his father was given a few weeks, but lasted months.

As we are all leaving, Dad opens his eyes. Once again I kiss my father on the forehead and say, "I love you, Dad. See you tomorrow." Once again, he says, "Love you, too."

We head for the elevator, but Bill goes back to the room. As he catches up with us at the elevator he is brushing moisture from his cheek. He is surprised by his own emotion.

"I had to say goodbye," he said. "I didn't expect to be so affected."

"What did you say?" I ask him.

"I need a brandy and maybe I'll tell you."

He hugs my mother in the hospital garage. "You're doing a great job!" he says. "He said goodbye to everyone. Trust me, you don't want to see it get worse."

I talk to Bill every day back in Florence. He's telling me he is doing great paintings and he's been invited to have a solo art show at a prestigious golf club. He tells me that we are invited to a party in two weeks at the castle of Nipozzano, the most cele- brated and historic property of the Frescobaldi fam- ily who are big wine producers in Tuscany.

"Sister Wendy Beckett, the international celeb- rity art critic, might be coming to Florence, and I re- ally want to meet her," he says. "When do you think you'll be back?"

I am pacing up and down the hall outside my father's room, talking on the cell phone. Bill says, "I'd like for you to be here for the show." He pauses before adding, "I just want to tell you I know what's happening, and I know how you are, and I know you can't leave, and I would do the same thing. It could go two months, and you may never get back here."

I look in at my dying father. *Do I choose life or death?*

I stay with my parents until my father passes away, then return to Florence in mid-November, glad to be back in the city that I'm starting to think of as home.

We attend the Frescobaldi engagement party at Nipozzano, the family's beautiful estate outside of Florence, a glorious place and a welcome distraction. The Castle Nipozzano was constructed around the year 1000 as a defensive stronghold; after reconstruction around the 1400s, the villa's cellars became the center of local wine production.

Today the castle, located on the top of a hill 350 meters high, houses the central wine cellars, where the production takes place. The castle is also the center of the hospitality and culinary programs of the Frescobaldi family. The property is in the heart of Chianti, stretching across of 1,359 acres: 395 acres cultivate the vines of Sangiovese, Cabernet Sauvignon, Cabernet Franc, Merlot, and Syrah.

We pick up Lisa and Marcello at Piazza Carmine in a taxi and arrive at this spectacular setting in less than an hour. Adults dressed in tweeds and woolens meander in and out of rooms filled with tables of food, as formally dressed, white-gloved waiters serve wine. Outside a giant barn fire roars, and young girls and boys dressed in Lederhosen run around. It is a scene from *The Sound of Music.*

As usual, Bill has brought along a small sketch-book, and this day would turn out to be the inspiration for two of his large, 5x6-foot landscapes, *Nipozzano* and *Tranquillo*.

—⊗—

On the day of the mid-term critique of students' artwork at Bill's school, he leaves shortly after eight while I am still sleeping. After the review, he goes with all "the kids" to the Old Post Irish Pub across the street from Florence's main post office for cele-bratory beers. We plan to meet in front of the Duomo and have dinner together.

It's dark as I walk across the Ponte Vecchio, along Via Por Santa Maria past Piazza del Mercato Nuovo and down toward the Piazza della Republica. It's a little past eight p.m.—just in time to wit-ness the shift change at the market. The last two wagons, fastened together and closed up with their wares securely inside, are crossing the street, leav-ing a vacant concrete slab that moments earlier had been a bustling market, filled with Florentines sell-ing leather bags, wallets, tablecloths, hats, scarves, postcards, and calendars.

As they head down the narrow Calimaruzza and across the Piazza della Signora to put their carts to bed for the night, they are instantly replaced by black men selling carved African statues, lighters, small wooden trains with alphabet letters, sunglasses, and knock–off designer bags. Soon they are set up in a line along the street.

A Senegalese man approaches with numerous handbags on either arm. *"Buonasera, signora,"* he says. I keep walking. I know from experience that the worst thing you can do is open a dialogue or make eye contact.

He follows nonetheless, speaking perfect English. "Excuse me, ma'am, English, American, French?" *"No, grazie,"* I say. *"Non mi piace"*—I don't like them. "I just want to show you the new Gucci collection," he says.

I am remembering Bill's story about coming back from Italy last year. One of these guys was in line in front of him at the ticket counter. He was flying to England business class, and he was paying with cash. These are handsome, articulate, and mostly educated men who speak five languages. Above all, they are amazing salesmen, and rarely lose a deal. "How much you want to pay?" he is saying as I leave his territory.

I have spoken with Bill only briefly today. He has told me that his art critique has demonstrated his obvious need for space. *He's had over a month alone. How much space does he need?* It brings to mind one of my tips from my first relationship book, *Why Men Commit*, which is based on a sales analogy. "Ninety percent of business is being there."

I break off half of a Xanax (pinched from my father's leftover medications) and stick it in my coat pocket in case Bill has some further revelations he wishes to share on the subject of space. This is likely to be the case following two hours of drinking beer. Over the phone he has also told me that the analysis of this recent body of work revealed, in addition to his need for space, that his feminine side is manifesting itself. I haven't seen much indication of this. Among other things, he still leaves the toilet seat up.

It's 8:45 p.m. I stand in front of the Duomo and alternate between giving directions and indulging couples who ask me if I will take a picture for them. It's a cool, but not freezing, December night. Many people are out walking. I always feel safe in Florence. The only real problem is gypsy pickpockets, who are fairly obvious, given their peasant dress. I wear my small black leather Coach bag, purchased expressly for travel, worn cross-body style like a Miss America sash.

Bill finally arrives and is quite thrilled with himself. He can't decide if he should rejoin "the kids" at the pub but since it is almost nine o'clock, I convince him we should have dinner. "We'll go to Il Bargello for pizza."

"No, let's try something different," I say.

After walking for a bit, we settle on an Osteria, Vini e Vecchi Sapori, "of wine and old flavors," a tiny restaurant, with only seven tables, on a side street off of Piazza della Signoria at Via de Magazinni 3. Usually there's a line outside but the first seating has departed, leaving a few vacant seats.

Bill catches his reflection in the window. "I think I've broken into a new dimension of 'ruggedly handsome.' I've given new meaning to the term," he says, as he pushes back his thinning blond hair, which is now too long and curling over his collar. As I thrust open the door, with no help from my self-proclaimed handsome husband, the owner, Mario, recognizes me. *"Signora autrice*, author," he exclaims, *"due minute."*

Mario is a robust character wearing a red apron and a chef hat. He stands in the middle of the room in about two square feet where he can hardly turn around, and he holds court, yelling orders over the counter. *"Una ribollita," "lasagne," "antipasto misto."* He clears the plates, talks to everyone, and periodically screams obscenities at the chef in the kitchen. No Americans are here. I count five tables of Italians, and next to us two young women from Madrid. Mario speaks Spanish to them, and then pulls one from her seat and dances with her in his tiny space. Everyone laughs and applauds.

Bill orders polenta with Bolognese sauce and beans, the special of the night. He leaves one bite. Mario, from his circular stage, asks him, "You don't like?" And Bill says, *"Splendido,"* rubbing his stomach to demonstrate that it is delicious, but he is full—*"pieno."* With the attention of all the patrons, Mario takes the last mouthful from the plate and feeds it to my husband. *"Finito!"* he says, and again comes laughter and cheers. No wonder everyone loves Italy and Italians.

———∞———

It is our second Thanksgiving in Italy. Lisa insists on making us a reservation at Harry's Bar. We are seated at the corner table in the front room— her "Grandmamma's table." It is brightly lit and across from a large table of New Yorkers, who tell us they are visiting their children, who are studying abroad in Florence. A sweet potato arrives, looking lonely on a plate. The next course is puree of potatoes, which are kind of soupy, and we can't get the turkey until we finish the other courses. How could we explain we want it all together, *tutto insieme*, on one plate, floating in a pool of gravy? It is the American turkey dinner but served Italian style, course by course. Next year, I promise myself, will be different.

———∞———

What I am shocked to discover in Florence is the culture of cattiness among the women. My first dose comes when Lisa invites us to a dinner party in Montacatini at the house of her American friend who is married to an Italian. Marcello is in a "mood" and decides not to go and Lisa needs a ride. As we do not have a car in Florence, Bill hires a driver who arrives in an ancient stretch Mercedes limousine.

We pick up Lisa in Piazza Carmine and head out of the city for our culinary adventure. We are looking forward to the dinner, because Lisa has told us that Ellen runs a cooking school at her house. Bill is happily anticipating a sumptuous Tuscan feast. "Ellen is absolutely the worst cook in the entire universe," Lisa says, as we drive off. "She serves cream cheese dip with Ritz crackers, if you can imagine."

Bill says, "Geez. I thought she was your best friend." Lisa says she *was* her friend and then tells us the entire story of the long affair carried on by Ellen's husband and how Ellen finally reconciled and went back with him. "Idiot," Lisa says. I feel uncomfortable that I have so much information when I am introduced to the unhappy but reconciled couple.

That night, in the glorious Tuscan farmhouse that has been in the family for generations, fireplaces are blazing in every room. Every inch of every wall is filled with old family portraits and oil paintings. Florentines are milling as we maneuver through the rooms and make conversation with some interesting characters.

Lisa is right about the food. The only appetizer consists of a block of Philadelphia cream cheese over which a bottle of chutney has been poured, then topped off with crumbled bacon and parsley, and surrounded by Ritz crackers. "What's that ad?" Bill says. "Everything tastes better when it sits on a Ritz?"

Dinner is a bright green jellied salad and a "Honey of a Ham" that someone recently brought over from America in their suitcase. We realize that Ellen must need a break from her genuine Italian cooking. Perhaps she thought this a rare treat for her mostly Italian audience. Despite ourselves, it made us just a bit homesick. Soon enough we would be back in the States for the Christmas holidays. We would not return to Italy until late August of 2001.

We had rented the same top-floor apartment on Lungarno Torrigiani, with its magnificent view of the Arno and the Uffizi Gallery across the river. Bill, now finished with school, has rented his first Florence studio in a building at the rear of the religious complex of San Marco, on Via Cavour, three blocks north of the Duomo. He has space on two floors (without phone or toilet), at the back of the cathedral in a building that has been converted to offices. It is located around the corner from the museum housing the major collection of works by Fra Angelico, a Dominican monk in the early 15th century, including his most renowned frescoes, *The Annunciation* and *The Adoration of the Magi*. Much of the monastery of San Marco remains untouched—where the brothers slept, prayed, painted, and studied.

I register for four hours a day of language studies at my school from two years ago, the Centro Ponte Vecchio. The staff and teachers remember me. I love this school even more in its new location in Piazza della Signoria, probably the most beautiful square in the world.

On our first free Sunday we take the train to Montecatini. We ride the small railway car —a little red train-- up the mountain to Montecatini Alto, which is the connection between the very old medieval village and the town below. It is one of the most ancient inhabited areas in Tuscany. We have a light lunch outside at La Torre marveling at the beauty of the day and the square. Later, we walk through the town enjoying the enchanting view of the valley.

───∞───

Back at work, Bill is happily immersed in a new 5x6-foot landscape from our time in Nipozzano, which he calls *Tranquillo*. This will become the cover of a book of his paintings.

I sign up for a cooking school, at Podere Le Rose, a beautiful 13th-century Italian farmhouse, surrounded by olive trees, in the heart of Chianti. It is run by the same two sisters who own and operate the language school in Florence that I attend, where I've made friends with a few of my classmates, who are from all over the world. I have come with Kimiyo, my Japanese friend from the language class, and "Linda-the-Loser," a recent divorcee in her 50s, who is largely interested in venting about her ex-husband. There was a couple in their 60s from Ohio and a man from Dublin in his early thirties.

We arrive to find the house has a huge kitchen, with a stone hearth and ovens. A colorfully attired Tuscan chef, Alvaro, complete with chef hat, white jacket with colored buttons, red bandana tied around his neck, and bright orange and green pants, is there to greet us for our first lesson and to provide us with a perfect photo opportunity.

We make *bruschette* of chopped fresh tomatoes with garlic, basil, olive oil, and vinegar, served on toasted slices of Italian bread; *tagliatelle ai fungi*, an egg noodle cut in long, flat strands, prepared with mushrooms; and *ravioli burro e salvia*, ravioli with butter and sage—both with the fresh pasta that we made and cut ourselves. The chef drinks wine the entire time and starts to add ingredients that are not called for in the recipe. He ends up drunk and the ravioli is in tomato sauce instead of butter and sage, but no one cares a bit.

After I return to Florence, Bill and I decide to plan a weekend in Venice. When I call American Express, at 3 pm, the travel agent tells me the World Trade Center is on fire. "The United States is under attack, do you have a TV?"

I turn it on and watch, horrified, as the second plane hits. I need to tell Bill. We have no cell phones, so he calls me each day at 4 p.m. from the café next to his studio. Thankfully, he calls earlier than usual, but he can barely understand what I am telling him. I'm not speaking clearly through my tears. "What?" he asks stunned. "Who died?"

He comes home and we start the phone calls. We are able to get through to our family members and find out that they are all okay, but we cannot leave the country; the airports are now closed. We have no Internet access at home, so we walk to the Internet café to read about what's going on and to send emails.

We spend the rest of the day switching channels among CNN, International CNBC, and the BBC. We can't get enough news from the U.S., and feel isolated not being home, not being able to help our country in some way. During the following days, still in shock, we follow the advice from George Bush to go on with our lives. I return to school, where several teachers express their fears that Florence is a target for terrorists because there are so many Americans here. They talk about the Duomo and the Uffizi being prime targets. They warn us not to dress like Americans.

Being in language class is a relief from watching the smoldering World Trade Center on TV. The inconceivable has occurred, and I find it nearly impossible to process what has happened. Bill seriously wonders if Navy intelligence will take him back— even now that he is in his late 50s.

Because we cannot go home, we stay and continue with life in Florence, Bill painting, me trying to learn Italian, and writing a story about my father. Florentines express their concern and eagerness to help, and American flags are displayed all over the city.

On Friday, September 14, I go to my conversation class at school for two hours. At noon, all the bells from surrounding churches ring out and we observe 3 minutes of silence for the people killed in the terrorist attacks. I feel overwhelming sadness for the U.S. and for the world.

We are expecting friends from the States who were to be visiting Florence in a few days, but we have no way to reach them. They can't get out of Italy, either, so they have continued with their trip and call us when they arrive at the Grand Hotel Villa Medici on Via il Prato, an elegant 18th-century villa, in the heart of Florence. Bill and I had stayed there in 1998 while looking at schools.

We invite them for drinks at our apartment, and we go back to their hotel for dinner at the Ristorante Lorenzo de' Medici, where we continue our conversation about the tragedy of 9/11 and our fear of repeat attacks. We are about to leave after dinner when we hear piano music coming from the bar, and it seems like a great idea to go in for a highly superfluous night cap. The piano player is happy to see two blonde American women in the not very crowded venue and invites us up to the stage as his backup singers. We end up joining him in his rendition of "Que Sera, Sera," the song that became Doris Day's signature. He sings a verse, then turns on his bench and nods to us and we join in the chorus;

> Que Sera, Sera,
> Whatever will be, will be
> The future's not ours, to see
> Que Sera, Sera
> What will be, will be.

He makes a taped copy, which he gives us, and we don't sound bad. I had a massive headache the next morning, but the message of the song had gotten through. I understand how useful fatalism can be if there is really nothing you can do to affect events.

The following day, the headline in the *International Herald Tribune* reads, "U.S Cautions Americans in Italy." The U.S. State Department says that it has received information about possible attacks on "symbols of American capitalism" in Italy in the next month and that Americans in that country should be cautious. "United States citizens and interests abroad continue to be at increased risk of terrorist actions from extremist groups," the department says.

I just hum, "What will be will be."

I can't get past the horror of 9/11. I've developed intestinal problems and am intimate with every restroom in the city. After three weeks, when the problem doesn't seem to be getting any better, I find the name of an English-speaking doctor through school. I call and make an appointment with Dr. Stephen Kerr, who is adorable and about the age of my children. He is English with the healthy good looks and perfect white teeth of Prince William. He instructs me to deliver a "specimen" to a medical laboratory, the Istituto Fanfani a Firenze in Piazza della Indipendenza, which will be my introduction to the Italian medical system.

On October 8, I start the new week by dropping off my "sample" at the lab. At my insistence Bill accompanies me. I have to wait until Thursday night to find out if I have salmonella, parasites, or E. coli. Bill urges me to not drink coffee and to stop watching the news. I walk home and the first thing I do is turn on CNN and find that an SAS plane has crashed into a Cessna in Milan. It's not a terrorist attack, spokespeople assure us. We are all so on edge.

All tests come back negative. I do not have parasites; it's nerves. My book, *The Second Time*

Around, is scheduled to come out in paperback in October, but the publishing industry, along with so much else, is in upheaval, and the tour is cancelled, my agent in New York informs me. It's a bad time to be selling a non-terrorist related book. There have been two articles in *USA Today* explaining how new books and book tours are being postponed, including another anticipated fall hardcover, *Plane Insanity,* about funny things that happen on airplanes.

We feel a need to get out of the city, so we rent a car for a drive to Tuscany to visit Bill's former art teachers, the internationally acclaimed South African artists Rose Shakinovsky and Claire Gavronsky (also known as the artist duo Rosenclaire.) Now retired as heads of the art department of the Lorenzo de' Medici School, they have started their own intensive residency study at La Cipressaia in Montagnana, which operates in the summer and fall.

They have invited us for tea at 4 p.m. I Google the directions and see that it is located 29 km (18 miles) from the city and the drive is estimated to take 36 minutes. We always add an extra hour when leaving Florence because of the gridlocked traffic, but today, miraculously, we get out faster than usual, and arrive in less than thirty minutes at Montagnana. It is surprising how fast we are transported to the peaceful countryside from the chaotic city.

With over an hour to spare we spot a sign at a cross street: Vinci 31 km (19 miles). We've always wanted to see the birthplace of Leonardo da Vinci—and here we are. "We have plenty of time," Bill says. We follow the occasional signs and eventually find the restored ancient stone dwelling surrounded by olive trees, in the town of Vinci, just outside its center on the foothills of Montalbano in a village called Anchiano. Here, Leonardo was born on April 15, 1452, an illegitimate child of a domestic servant and Piero da Vinci, owner of the house at that time. We are thrilled to be here.

We get lost on the way back to our original destination. Bill doesn't have the phone number or the actual address. What he does have is a hand drawn map with notations that say things like, "go up the hill, over the river and take the fork on the left." We can't find a fork. I'm just glad it's not me without a phone number or decent directions.

At my insistence, he finally agrees to stop an oncoming car and ask the *polizia* for help. Eventually we arrive, 45 minutes behind schedule, at the 18th-century spacious Tuscan farmhouse. It is located on a private hilltop surrounded by cypresses, olive trees, and grapevines deep in the Chianti countryside.

The women pop open a bottle of Prosecco, serve us cheese and crackers, and tell us excitedly about a spa they have just returned from. When I share my intestinal predicament, they insist we should also go to Bagno Vignoni and they tell us we should stay at the Hotel Posta Marcucci and experience the healing waters that date back to the Middle Ages. Claire calls the hotel for us and attempts to make a reservation for the weekend but they are booked. The girls gang up on Bill and tell him that to an artist, a weekend is *anytime*. I, of course, agree because I want to bathe in the hot volcanic waters. I'll try anything if there is a possibility of it making me better. Bill agrees and we are booked for Thursday. My editor for *The Second Time Around*, Betty Kelly Sargent of William Morrow Publishers, has a house close by in San Quirico d'Orcia, and she has also recommended the spa.

A week later, we arrive at our hotel in the Tuscan countryside amidst the rolling hills and fields in the Val d'Orcia. We are here to "take the cure," with an added bonus of Bill getting new artistic inspiration; the colors surrounding us, brilliant yellows, reds and violets are dazzling.

Terrycloth robes and slippers await us in the room. We change into our bathing suits and head to the hot thermal baths-- enjoyed by the Romans before us and the Etruscans before them. We stand, waist deep, among a diverse group of men and women—some wearing shower caps-- waiting to be cured of everything from aching bones to nervous stomachs. It's all very relaxing as the steam floats above the baths.   But when I leave two days later, I am still not cured.

Life Goes On

By October, we're finding life more frustrating than charming. Our safe haven for bill paying and travel planning the American Express office on Via Dante Alighieri, is now under armed protection. Bulletproof glass protects and separates the employees from the clients. Guards with security scanners stand at the entrance door and take great delight in running the scanners over the front of large-bosomed women. Then they look at each other and practically collapse in suppressed hysterical laughter. My friend and travel agent Graciela works here, and we used to have the occasional lunch, but now she is frightened and wants to quit her job.

Some of my clothes are now hanging off me and I have bought a new pair of black pants that fit but need to be shortened. I call Suzanne, our friend and rental agent, and ask for the name of a seamstress.

I follow her directions but cannot find her tailor, as I have no actual address, so I ask in a few stores. It takes over an hour to find the place, because it has no name, and isn't visible from the street, since it is on the second floor.

"*Parla inglese?*" I ask, when I arrive, at last.

"A little," the woman says. I demonstrate that I want the slacks shortened and I duck behind the counter and put them on. I put heels on, so she will know how much to shorten them. She leans over turns up a cuff on one leg and aimlessly sticks a pin in one leg of the pant.

"*Mi scusi,*" I say. "*Avete uno specchio interno?*" (Do you have a mirror?) I want to see the length. "No" she says, as she turns and goes back to her sewing table. What are the chances of this turning out to my satisfaction? Slim to none, as Bill would say.

One week passes and I cross the Ponte Vecchio, walk past Coin department store to Matucci and turn right, onto via Del Corso, past Paoli restaurant, and climb the stairs to the no-name seamstress to pick up my altered black pants. I pay the equivalent of $7 for the alteration. But the low price only adds to my anxiety about the workmanship.

On the way home, I buy some cheese and grapes and wholegrain bread for our cocktail hour, when Bill will return from his studio and we will discuss the day's events and watch what's new in terrorism on CNN.

I immediately put on the newly shortened black pants. They are two inches too short, and cropped pants were not the rage at this time. Whatever happened to the great tradition of Italian tailoring?

Bill wants to go to Bargello for dinner and sit outside. He says it's a beautiful night and we won't have many more like it. He says the exact same thing every night. I want to stay home—near my toilet. So, we walk down the street and get 2 pizzas, one Margherita and one Fuego, (spicy) at Runner Time, the take out place, and bring them home. We eat our pizza in front of the TV and watch a Seinfeld episode dubbed in Italian at 7:30 on Channel 21. "I'm so glad I decided to stay home," Bill says. "Every now and then, you just have to stay home." "Absolutely," I nod.

My cultural challenges continue. I go to Coin department store to buy a fitted sheet for our bed. The sizes of the beds are different here than in the States, where there is the simple queen or king size; the saleswoman gives me a *matrimonia* size and says it is the standard size and will fit all the beds in the city. It does not fit, so I return it to the store. The standard bed size in Italy is basically a queen size. We have what would be a king size because it is two twin beds hinged together.

This is the day I learn that there are no returns in Italy. The woman just keeps repeating in Italian that I bought it, so I must have wanted it. I refuse to leave until she agrees to exchange it for the correct size. Score one for America's retail mantra, "The customer is always right." I even returned a chicken in Florence once because I thought it smelled funny. And that was a real feat, because the Italians do not comprehend the concept of returning anything, so it becomes the ultimate challenge accompanied by a great sense of accomplishment.

Ciao Pussy

Being in Florence during and after 9/11 exposed us to the warmth and compassion of our Italian friends. They have a poignant word for this: *simpatico*. We begin to feel a true connection to these sympathetic people, and thus allow ourselves to be captivated by some truly amazing characters.

Lisa has lived in Florence for 40 years, and she also owns a villa in Positano that was re-designed by Marcello. She is planning a seventieth birthday party for him there on Halloween weekend, but she isn't sure if he would show up; theirs is a complicated, mysterious relationship. She invites us to accompany her and stay as her guests and be part of the birthday celebration. Lisa knows everybody who's anybody in Positano, and she has a busy schedule set up for us.

The three of us will take the Eurostar fast train from Florence to Rome, a trip of less than two hours. We book the 12:55 train and make a lunch reservation. After boarding, we check our seats and go directly to the dining car. The food is good enough, as is the wine, and the time passes in a pleasant blur of scenery.

From Rome to Naples is another two hours. Our friend and driver, Mimi, who was responsible for our meeting Lisa, picks us up at the train station and drives to Lisa's villa. On the way, he stops at the mozzarella factory in Sorrento and buys us several large mounds of the freshly made cheese. He pulls a few leaves off a basil plant and selects two large ripe tomatoes at a roadside vegetable stand along the twisting coastal road. Mimi says, getting back in the car, *"Chi va piano, va sano e va lontano!"* Lisa translates: "Who goes slowly, goes in good health and goes a long way!"

Positano is the Amalfi coast's most picturesque and photogenic town. Perched vertically on the face of a cliff dotted with pastel colored houses, the town winds its way down to the water. It began as a fishing village but today is one of Italy's most romantic and luxurious vacation spots, a small walking town with many stairs.

Lisa's villa is pale pink stucco with a forest green wrought-iron gate and white doors. The walls are practically hidden behind pink and purple bougainvillea spilling over the patio. The view of the sea from every window is breathtaking. A large entrance hall opens to a living room to the left, and a dining room to the right that leads to a pantry, kitchen, and half-bath. Upstairs are four bedrooms and three more bathrooms. Two of the bedrooms, including ours, have balconies overlooking the Amalfi coast. Even Lisa describes the view as "stupendous."

Two kittens we dubbed Tom and Jerry, always on the prowl for food, live at the villa. They sleep together, one's head on the other's body, their paws intertwined adorably. Tom and Jerry get into the mozzarella the first night. They push it off the counter, and I find it on the floor the next morning with teeth marks. We will have to buy something else for lunch.

Maria, the maid, comes every day and cooks lunch, an easy job for her—only three people in a house that sleeps eight, and we go out every night for dinner. Lisa says the pasta and pizza are superior in Positano because of the local spring water. "Coffee is better, too." She is right.

The first day Maria makes small meatballs, called *polpette*. The consistency is so light and delicate that when I place one in my mouth, it seems to dissolve the moment it makes contact with my tongue, and begs to be washed down with the local red wine we drink every day at lunch. I ask her to write down the recipe for me. She serves them along with pasta and a piquant homemade tomato sauce.

Still not sure if the birthday boy will materialize, we are invited to Lisa's friends' house for a cocktail party. Maura, the hostess, somewhere around age 70, is Irish and is living with her considerably younger Italian gigolo. Her first words to us upon introduction are, "You Americans invited 9/11. It was your own fault." On that note, Bill and I decide to leave, as does Lisa. We call a cab and depart.

Marcello does arrive the day of the planned celebration and Lisa invites her entire "Positano posse" for the birthday dinner—with the exception of Maura. A handsome guy is talking about being on the *Johnny Carson Show* and playing golf with Clint Eastwood and George Bush. Bill asks, "Who are you?" He turns out to be *Robocop* actor Peter Weller. Bill stays up till the wee hours talking to Robocop, who has a house in Positano, and is in the process of earning a Master of Fine Art at Syracuse University in Florence.

A woman whom Lisa has described as having had a bad facelift and silicone injections that make her look like Mickey Mouse's dog, Pluto, was also there. Upon meeting her, I vow to never have plastic surgery. Her face looks as though it had melted like a cartoon character's. With Lisa there is always a diverse group, and this party is no exception. There was a delightful gay couple from New York with an extra lover—the pair and a spare.

Dinner is served buffet style: gateau of potatoes, fried anchovies, and a salad. Everyone stands around trying to figure out how to balance a plate, eat, talk, and drink. My favorite member of the "posse" is Fifi, a woman from Turkey who claims she is a princess. The ladies present refer to her as "Ciao

Pussy" when she is out of earshot. Her real name sounded something like Chafica, and *fica* translates to "fig" in Italian—or a very crude slang for a woman's private parts, hence the acquired nickname. The middle-aged, heavily made-up Fifi uses very dark eyeliner and fills in her lips with an intense shade of purple, giving her a somewhat sinister appearance. She is attired in tight gold silk pants and a transparent black blouse displaying a set of unusually large nipples—a spectacle, ogled by the men around her. Ropes of shiny gold beads are wrapped around her neck and fall at different levels on her chest, performing a glittery, mesmerizing dance and keeping the focal point where it is intended to be.

When the party ends and it is time to leave Positano we suggest the train, but Lisa insists on the car. Lisa, Marcello, Bill, and I squish into Mimi's Mercedes and we are off to Florence. First stop is Sorrento to pick up fresh buffalo mozzarella. Lisa is carrying a bunch of fresh sage given to her by her maid, Maria. We drive for a few hours before stopping in Frascati, outside of Rome, for lunch at Ristorante Cacciani. The weather is perfect, and we are led to a large round table on the terrace where we dine on traditional Roman cooking and drink delicious white wine, a specialty of the region, from the vineyard next door.

Three more hours to Florence and we are sleepy from the wine. During the drive, we make a deal with

Lisa to rent her villa for a month the following September; the terms are cash plus a painting of the villa.

⸎

Back in Florence, I receive an email from my son saying he is coming for a visit, alone. His wife and two-year-old will not be traveling with him. I find this strange, as we are in a war atmosphere and he has decided to fly across the ocean, leaving his family behind. Bill thinks he is coming with a message that he's getting a divorce. I don't know what to think. I'll just take it whatever comes as it comes, and enjoy his company and visit. I will be happy to have the opportunity to walk down the streets in Florence with my son, take him to the museums, and introduce him to the wonderful food. Que sera, sera.

He asks if there's anything I need that he can bring. There is no Pepto Bismol in Italy, nothing containing red food dye is allowed, the pharmacist tells me. I think I have bought up all the Immodium in Florence at this point and it's not working. I have moved to Maalox Plus, and that doesn't work either. My mother tells me only Pepto Bismol will work, because it is healing. So my son arrives and brings it in every form: pills, liquid, and lozenges. I start to feel better almost immediately. We have a wonderful visit and there is no news of marital conflict. *Tutto bene!*

Several weeks after he leaves, growing tired of the cold and rainy weather, I return to Florida in mid-November. Bill stays in Florence and we meet in Boston for Christmas.

Bill accepts an invitation to do another art show at The Walter Wickiser Gallery in New York City In April 2002, not expecting anything much, so soon after 9/11. But New York is getting back on its feet. *Riflessioni Italiane* (Italian Reflections), featuring the 5x6-foot painting of Nipozzano, along with the collection from the previous autumn in Florence, is a big success.

Amalfi

We have rented Lisa's villa in Positano for the month of September, 2002. We fly directly to Rome, and Mimi picks us up and drives us, once again stopping at the mozzarella factory in Sorrento, but this time insisting we go inside with him to meet his friends.

We pull into the curve of Grotta di Fornillo in Positano — a bus stop—to unload. I have brought three oversized body bags. "How the hell are you going to get those up all the stairs?" Bill asks. "Maybe finally you will learn to pack light." I bite my tongue and don't say, "We will be in Italy for four months. How can I pack light?"

Immediately, two gorgeous, bronzed muscular men appear—one of whom had to be named Fabio: "*Buon giorno, Signora. Prego?* May I?" Each grabs a suitcase and flings it over his shoulder. I follow them up the stairs to the villa but only after I turn and offer a smug wink at Bill. They tell us they work for the hotel next door as porters.

Lisa will take the train down the next day to make sure we were settled and to make a few social engagements and reintroduce us to her friends. We've been invited by her good friend Anna Sersale for lunch. Lisa wants to have a glass of wine before lunch at Buca di Bacco on the beach. She tells us she loves to go there on Sunday and watch the promenade along the waterfront. It is 11 a.m. when Bill and Lisa order wine; I stick with mineral water. As we are about to toast, I hoist my glass, but Lisa tells me it brings bad luck to toast with water, so just she and Bill clink glasses. *"Salute!"*

Italian at-table etiquette requires keeping both hands in sight on the table. I ask why, when in America we are taught the opposite. Lisa says that this is true in all of Italy, especially Sicily; both hands must be visible at all times because, "You can't have a knife under the table if both hands can be seen." When she accidentally knocks over her glass, she tells us that spilling red wine is good luck. She proceeds to dip her finger in the wine and dab some behind her ear, then Bill's and mine. "Spilling olive oil is bad luck."

Lisa says she is getting a cold and you shouldn't go in the sun with a cold. "I have the cure," Bill says with a note of genuineness. "Echinacea, red wine, and lots of sex." I cringe, but fortunately she laughs. I can't figure out how he can get away with the things he does and says. "Italians say you shouldn't go in the sun during any month that has the letter R," she continues. I hope I can remember all these Italian superstitions.

Lunch is scheduled at the Hotel Sirenuse, hosted by Anna Sersale, who along with her brother Franco is the proprietor of the hotel. The family lived in Naples and this was originally their summer home. The lunch is primarily a welcome for the new American Consul General to Naples.

The Sireneuse is an exquisite luxury boutique hotel, overlooking the sea and the Duomo, and furnished with a mixture of antiques and modern comforts. Chairs are covered in pure white with azure piping, and the floors are tiled in white with an occasional pattern. Almonds that are toasted at the hotel daily are served with cocktails. Anna tells us that if we eat nine almonds a day, we will have flawless skin.

At 88 years old, Anna is sharp, witty, fashionable, and incredibly charming. She tells us about her recent travels to Pakistan, India, and China. I decide I want to be just like Anna when I'm in my 80s. Lisa tells her that a man Anna hasn't seen in 40 years is coming to Positano to see her. "Well, he's in for a big shock," Anna chuckles. She is old and tanned and wrinkled and absolutely delightful. She insists that Bill be seated next to her.

Lunch is over at 4 p.m. and we head back to the villa. By the time we arrive, Bill and I decide to walk down the 500 steep steps along the path that leads to the Fornillo Beach and the Bar Pupetto while Lisa takes a nap.

For dinner, we stay home and Maria makes a feast. Somewhere around midnight I leave Bill and Lisa repeating the same stories. I choose sleep over the wine-induced dialogue that is now making very little sense.

Lisa only stays a few days, and when she leaves we are on our own. Bill fills his days painting the magnificent sights of the cliffs of Positano stretching into the aqua blue waters of the Mediterranean and the Emerald Grotto. We go up the hill to Montepertuso where Bill sets up his easel and paints. Schoolchildren, wearing backpacks on their way home, surround him and watch in awe. Following lunch, I sit and write on the terrace at La Tagliata restaurant, a spectacular location with its helicopter view of the Galli Isles, Capri and Positano below.

"Ischia...dove si mangia si beve e si fischia!" (To Ischia, where they eat, they drink and they whistle!)

A friend of ours, a young chef in Sarasota, Gianluca Di Costanzo, is from Ischia, the most developed and largest of the three islands off the coast of Naples, the other two being Procida, and Capri. His parents, who live there, have invited us to visit.

Raffaele Di Costanzo, a retired teacher and a sculptor, wants to meet Bill, a fellow- artist. Gianluca has given his father a book of Bill's paintings. Raffaele will meet us at the boat and we will recognize him, because he will be carrying the book.

The ferryboat ride, with a stop in Capri takes about one and a half hours on this beautiful, sun-drenched day. When we spot the gorgeous island, rising from the sapphire waters of the Tyrrhenian Sea in the Bay of Naples, Bill says, "I have to paint this." We dock at the Port of Ischia and right away spot a man, who looks younger than us, holding up the identifying book; we greet each other and embrace like old friends.

Raffaele, takes us for a brief tour of the gorgeous island and then to his house for lunch. There, awaiting us is his wife Tina, slender and trim, with short dark hair, wearing a sleeveless housedress. She has been preparing a mouth-watering lunch and serves us spaghetti pomodoro, eggplant parmesan, and, when we are completely stuffed, veal Milanese. We eat, drink wine, and converse as best we can in Italian, as they speak no English. "Mama Tina," as Bill starts to call her, will not allow us to help in the clean-up. We have been invited to stay over, but I scan the house and cannot imagine where we would sleep—*and* there is only a single bathroom.

We pass the afternoon chatting and enjoying the company of these lovely people—then it is time for dinner. This time Raffaele takes us to a different town, Serrara Fontana, and we drive up a steep hill until we arrive at a breathtaking, panoramic view from one of the highest points on the island, at 1800 feet.

Ristorante Bracconiere, with its lively atmosphere looks like a saloon from an old American Western. A wagon wheel hangs on the wall in a room of long tables with benches, red checked table clothes, and green and pink hanging lamps. Salvatore Di Meglio, a family friend and chef, prepares a delicious dinner of traditional Ischian cuisine, including rabbit and abundant appetizers, accompanied by three liters of wine and limoncello, the lemon-flavored after-dinner drink made from the extraordinary lemons grown on the Amalfi coast. When we can eat and drink no more, a confident Raffaele, takes the wheel, elbows wide, over steering, barely averting the headlights coming at us, with the car stalling periodically in the pitch dark as he drives back down the forbidding zigzag hill, with all of us laughing and singing "Volare." And we are definitely flying.

He pulls up in front of a butcher shop, gets out, and opens the door for me. I take my tote bag and get out as he leads us across the street to what looks like a new but uninhabited motel. His relative owns this place, he explains—at least, that is our interpretation of what we think he says as he turns the key and unlocks the door to lovely mini apartment with a large bedroom and a kitchenette.

"*Come è bello* (how beautiful)," Bill says. I ask, "*Dove è possibile un cappuccino al mattino?* "Oh no," Raffaele says, "*Io verrò* (I will come)." Then he closes the door and locks it behind him. So here we are, locked in a room on a remote Mediterranean island, having consumed too much wine; we can't escape and we have no cell phone. *Who would find us if no one came? Who would tell our children? What if there was a fire?*

We awake at dawn to the sounds of roosters. Raffaele arrives to retrieve us at nine in the morning, as promised. He drives us to a seaside café for breakfast before taking us to the boat. He does not want us to leave. Big hugs and kisses on both cheeks are followed by promises to meet again—perhaps in America. We hope so. As the boat pulls away from the dock, we turn to see Raffaele salute us. Bill salutes back and I shed a few tears. We sit down on the bench and Bill starts to whistle.

Our friends Bob and Katherine from Sarasota are coming for the week. Bill's best friend from Sarasota, Brian Johnson, AC/DC lead singer, is in England. He calls and says he's by himself in London and wants to join the fun. He arrives the same night. There are two suites in the villa, one of which is ours, so Brian is relegated to a maid's room. He is so easy and so much fun and he doesn't care a bit. When we're together we usually laugh non-stop, because if Brian wasn't in the band, he could definitely have a career as a stand-up comedian.

Brian and my husband are cut from the same cloth, an ocean and three-and-a-half years apart. One is a rock star and the other an artist. Brian is a collector of my husband's paintings, and we have gone to Brian's concerts, visited his home in Newcastle, where he was born, and know his entire family. Both of their fathers fought against the Germans in the Battle of Anzio in 1944, cause for an indelible bond between their sons.

We go to a nearby restaurant, Mediterraneo, for dinner; which is also the name of our favorite restaurant in Sarasota. Bill introduces Bob to Renzo the owner. Bob is hard of hearing. "Ginzo," he says, "Nice to meet you."

The next morning we take the long and winding road from the villa to town. We want to show our friends the town of Positano and take them for lunch at La Cambusa. We are seated on the patio, overlooking the beach with a perfect view to watch the fisherman arrive with nets full of freshly caught fish. After a hypnotic, long, and leisurely afternoon we head home.

Once again, with Bill "knowing the city like the back of his hand," we board a bus to go back up the steep hill to our villa, but since it is going in the opposite direction, we end up at the San Pietro Hotel. We had planned to show our friends how beautiful it is, so we are not unhappy. Bill recognizes a tall, handsome guest of the hotel as, "Lute" Olson, a retired American men's basketball coach most recently head coach at the University of Arizona for twenty-five years. So he approaches him and starts a conversation about the current college basketball teams (my husband is a sports encyclopedia) and introduces Lute to the much shorter Brian, who comes up to Lute's waist. It is a great photo opportunity. Lute is with several other Americans who are there for his son's wedding. So we stay for a few hours and chat before taking a taxi back to the villa.

Bill continues his work routine and paints the views from Lisa's villa and the Amalfi coast daily. I wander the narrow streets and return to Ceramica Assunta on Via C. Colombo and order charming hand-painted Vietri dishes to ship back to the States. I am drawn to child-like plates in white with borders of red, orange, green, and shades of blue featuring hand-painted cows, pigs, dogs, elephants or horses around the border. I choose a variety of colors and patterns with coordinated solid color bowls and bread plates. A table set with these artistic handmade ceramics has the effect of a kid's birthday party—colorful and happy.

Maria comes to cook lunch every day. Her food is delectable and she happily gives me the recipes. (See Recipes chapter at end of book for some of her best dishes.)

The month is up too soon and we head back to Florence. Brian arrives in Florence and decides to look for a property. We house hunt with him, then it's back to work for both of us. In November, I return to Sarasota to look for a house.

The "Relationship Expert"

September 2003: my daughter is expecting her first child, and I want to be there soon after the birth. Actually, I wanted to be at the birth, but this is not what she wanted, understandably, I admit.

Bill leaves for Florence and our same apartment, but finds a new studio on Via de Tornabuoni, the city's chicest shopping street. He tells me his studio is on the top floor of an office building directly across the street from the picturesque *Chiesa dei Santi Michele e Gaetano,* the church of San Gaetano.

I stay in Florida and await the birth. I'm beginning to wonder how to stay married, with all the separations and our lives going in such different directions. I am experiencing the typical conflicts of women being pulled in every direction. I return to Florence mid-October and we reconnect.

After three years in the same apartment, Bill tells me he's thinking about spending more time in Italy. He wants to buy a place in Florence or do an annual lease. I realize I have to decide whether to stay in Florence or even stay married. I love the city and being surrounded by art. I love my husband and miss him when we are apart. Who else would remember what year we did anything? My children are functioning without me, and so is my widowed mother; they do not need me. My book tours are over at the moment and I can work on a new book in Italy with few distractions. *Isn't this what I always wanted—to live in a foreign country?*

We decide to take a trip to Bellagio in the end of October. I book the Grand Hotel Villa Serbelloni at the recommendation of friends who honeymooned there. We take the train from Florence and then a passenger ferry on Lake Como and arrive at our destination, a splendid Old-World hotel.

Our spacious room with terrace overlooks Lake Como with magnificent views of the Alps. Here we can discuss future plans uninterrupted. It's cold and the season is coming to a close, so there are few guests at the hotel.

We venture out on a rainy walk to Bellagio's main town square, Piazza San Giacomo, lined with shops and cafes, many already closed for the season. I stop to buy some waterproof, black oxfords that look like they are the latest fashion for nuns. The town church, the Romanesque Basilica di San Giacomo, dominates the square. On the opposite side of the square is a medieval tower. At this point a paved footpath (signposted) leaves the road and heads towards Pescallo, about ten minutes by foot. This is an enchanting little fishing village looking out over the western branch of Lake Como, on the opposite side of the peninsula from the main settlement of Bellagio. Bill imagines painting the colorful wooden boats pulled up on shore.

We return to the hotel to shower for dinner, and Bill heads for the bar while I get dressed. I find him engaged in conversation with the only other couple in sight. Bill opened the discussion about a book he had recently finished, *Up Country*, by Nelson DeMille. The man, who is with his wife on their honeymoon, starts to tell a riveting story about stealing a Buddha from a temple when he was in Vietnam during the war. He lived with the guilt for many years until he decided that he would go back, find the temple, and return the Buddha. Bill invites them to join us for dinner in the hotel dining room so we can hear the rest of the story, which his new wife is hearing for the first time. How true it is that being away from home opens people up in new and unexpected ways.

Buy or Rent?

We discuss and re-discuss the move until I am convinced, and in May of 2004, having made the decision for total immersion, we fly back to Florence with a new understanding, at first thinking we will buy a small house or condo and stay for most of the year.

"I'm not a renter," Bill says, "We should buy something."

We look in Florence but nothing is right for us in the city. We know we do not want a renovation project. We research sales and learn that when prime city properties become available, they are offered to the old Florentine families: Ferragamo, Frescobaldi, Antinori, Corsini, to name a few. These families have been around for hundreds of years and they own most of the property in the center of the city. Prices are high, and it is virtually impossible to find something reasonable.

Our real estate agent, Suzanne's son Corso, now in business with his mother, is in charge of sales. He suggests we look in Fiesole, an, upscale residential hilltop town five miles north of Florence; a 20-minute ride by car or the number 7 bus, which leaves from Via La Pira, very close to Piazza San Marco.

On a bright, crisp day, Corso picks us up and drives us to a simple three-bedroom house that overlooks Florence, with stunning views. Stray dogs run around the property, and there are bicycles and scooters in front. We learn there are no property title searches in Italy. The house was left to the children of the owners, but one son decided he didn't want to sell his share, and has kept a bedroom. The front porch has an easement, so that all of the relatives of the surrounding houses can use it. "No, thanks," I say.

Corso suggests that it could be a very positive experience—"a real bonus"—to share the porch if we like the people. I turn to walk down the steps and trip over a tricycle.

We have friends who own a lovely restored farmhouse in Chianti. They are constantly being broken into by gypsies, who have even stolen their newly installed security system. They advise us against buying. We hear some horror stories about the government coming after people for past taxes that a previous owner hadn't paid. We get talked out of buying by just about all the Americans we know who live in Florence.

So, we look at rentals in the city center for a couple of weeks with Suzanne and narrow the choice down to five apartments. Bill and I agree ahead of time that we will not give our final opinion until we have seen them all, but as soon as we enter the third apartment I know it is *the one*. Located inside one of Florence's designated historic buildings, it has a charming entry courtyard, complete with fountain and frescos. From the courtyard, access to "our" apartment is by elevator or five flights of stairs. We will share the top floor, with only one other apartment.

We see the remaining apartments but Bill and I agree on Palazzo Tanagli, at 27 Borgo degli Albizi, without question. We will be living in an elegant and quiet restored *cinquecento* building in the Duomo area. Built around 1500, it has been completely updated and renovated, with three pristine bedrooms and three bathrooms. During the refurbishing, original frescoes from Pompeii were discovered in the master bedroom, and all work had to stop until the paintings were restored, in obedience to Italian law.

In Florence, we have been constantly surrounded by art, and now will even sleep with it. Excitedly, we sign a two-year lease with a two-year option starting the following September. We are now free to enjoy our remaining time in Florence and Tuscany.

We take off with David, our friend and driver, to discover a place to hide out, work, and relax. I am in the process of writing a novel about dealing with the death of my father. We drive to nearby Chianti and the surrounding towns, scouting possibilities where Bill can paint.

My vote is for Castellina in Chianti, which is our last stop. Locanda Le Piazza, a rustic, but elegant country inn, dating from 1540, is the perfect spot for David to leave us on our own for a few days. It is truly off the beaten path. As we exit the main road and drive up a rocky dirt hill past acres of vineyards, we are in for a spectacular surprise. Several stone farmhouses have been recently converted to a small hotel and seem to glow in the golden light. All the elements are here; it is charming, picturesque and romantic. Bill exclaims, *"Bella vista."*

We enter our villa, with its oversized furnishings by Ralph Lauren, covered in bright beautiful fabrics. Vases of fresh flowers are everywhere and the views from the windows over the Tuscan landscape, with its terraced vineyards and dark cypresses, are spectacular. We ask David to pick us up in several days, but having no car turns into a definite disadvantage.

This charming guesthouse is owned by a woman of English/Irish heritage. On our first night, we look forward to dinner in the beautiful dining room, but it is shockingly awful. So, here we are in Tuscany with no car in a tastefully restored farmhouse with, mysteriously, a Jamaican chef, who can't cook. The dining room is staffed by a single waiter, who more often than not seems annoyed or at least over-whelmed by the demands of the tourists.

The second day, I write outside and Bill paints contentedly, his easel balanced on the grass, over-looking vineyards in their orderly rows. And so, we pass the days peacefully working, ensconced on this beautiful property, despite bad food. We leave happily looking forward to returning to Florence and some good Tuscan cooking.

The Expatriates

In September, fully committed to our life in Florence, we move into our magnificently furnished apartment in Palazzo Tanagli, a narrow cobblestone street, two blocks from the Duomo. We so loved the place when we first saw it, we had not noticed there were no carpets and only a tiny television. We invest in a flat screen TV and find a store selling Persian rugs. We keep looking for the perfect rug for the living room, but each time we lug one home it doesn't work, so it goes in the hall or a bedroom. We end up buying 6 handsome carpets, none for the living room.

Although the green and white marble bathrooms are new, I had forgotten that the showers look like something out of the '70's Woody Allen movie *Sleeper*— a Plexiglas orgasmatron with a clear plastic window in front. You step in to the small circular, stand-up unit and roll the door closed around yourself. There is an overhead hand- held shower and jets that shoot the water out with such force that it feels like nails hitting your back.

Upstairs is a studio/loft with a desk where I can write. It opens to a tiny deck with a bistro table and two chairs; a room with a view—a room at the top. Life is all so perfect as I gaze out over the rooftops, recording our lives here. Perhaps there will be a plaque outside at some future point, stating that the artist William Kelley and the writer Susan Kelley lived here from the years 2004 to...?

The second day of our new life as expatriates, we meet our next-door neighbors, retired American attorneys from New York. They hear us unlock our door, about three feet from theirs, and pop their heads out, introducing themselves. She is a petite athletic woman, around my age, with short hair, sweatpants, and a gorgeous toothy smile. Her handsome husband stands just behind her, chuckling, "If you need any help with anything, Laura is the expert." We cannot believe our good fortune; it is love at first sight.

———

Sometimes, Laura and I go for days without seeing each other. Other times we are on the phone four times a day and Bill comes in and says, "She's next door, why are you on the phone?" So I knock on her door, phone in hand, and we stand in the hall talking on the phone. Bill starts to call us Lucy and Ethel.

Laura is almost fluent in Italian and even reads books in the language. She invites me to her weekly women's language group.

I join the International League, a group of English speaking women, at the suggestion of my new friend and neighbor. I re-sign up for stretching and toning class at the Florence Dance Center on Borgo Stella founded and directed by Keith Ferrone, a New York choreographer, and his Italian former ballerina wife, Marga Nativo. I meet him through Lisa, whom Keith had helped with rehab after she'd had two hip replacements.

I enroll in Italian classes at Instituto Dante Alighieri at the nearby Piazzale Porta al Prato. After all, Dante Alighieri is the father of the Italian language. I am going to study two weeks of Italian, four hours a day.

The class starts at 9 a.m., which is a problem, as Bill doesn't want me to set an alarm clock or otherwise awake him. I walk to the language school to register and fill out the forms, including date of birth. *Come on, do they really need to know the year?* I fudge the year. The woman takes the information, we sign the forms and I give her my credit card. She says, "Too bad you're not a little older, we give 20% discount if you are 55 or over. "I am!" "No, the date you wrote says you are not yet fifty five." "I lie about my age." She laughs. Now we have the attention of everyone in the office of the school looking at me to see if I look over 55. I promise her I will bring my passport on Monday before class. The word for discount is *sconto*. It is my favorite Italian word.

We get WiFi installed and purchase all the necessary household items at the newly opened IKEA store in a warehouse-like space on Via Francesco Redi. We need a dresser, so I take a taxi to the store and arrive home with a large flat box. Bill looks at the box, which does not compute to *large piece of furniture*. The problem? It is "unassembled," in about a thousand pieces. He stares at the open box in complete horror. "No fucking way am I putting that together."

Several months pass, the box remains in the same place, and I have a brilliant idea. I write a note and slip it under Portis and Laura's door: "Dresser assembly party, 5 p.m., Sunday. Come as you are and bring tools; wine and food served."

Sure enough, they arrive on schedule with screwdrivers and a hammer, and Portis is an absolute whiz at the process of assembly. The boys work side by side for three hours until the raw pine chest with four drawers is complete and standing.

We become Monday night regulars at the Odeon Movie theatre, where current films are screened in their original language—with Italian subtitles. Built in 1462, Palazzo Strozzino, the building in which the cinema is located, is considered one of the most interesting example of Renaissance architecture. This elegant art nouveau cinema-theatre was opened in 1922. It is yet another jewel in the heart of Florence.

Laura and Portis have lived here for two years; they are fully immersed by the time of our arrival. They know the system and how to get things done. At their suggestion, we team up, hoping for a better price, and have screens installed on several of our windows. With screens in our bedroom, we can now sleep peacefully, minus the buzz and bites of the dreaded *zanzare,* mosquitoes.

In the spring, we rent a car and take a trip to Il Borro, a restored village in Tuscany, a whole town with its own tiny plaza, artisan shops, boutiques, church, cobbler, goldsmith, restaurant, delicatessen and wine bar, owned by the Ferragamo family. Here we find a hand-made rocking chair for Bill. Somehow we fit it sideways in the back seat and make it back to the Hertz garage, where we transfer it to a taxi. Borgo degli Albizi is becoming a cozy, personalized home.

We find the name of an English speaking computer "expert" through our rental agency. He arrives but is more interested in taking photos from our rooftop, which is his "passion." When he connects the router box, we are so excited about our new access to the

Internet that we don't notice till hours later that the phone no longer works. For an American living in Florence, the most important virtue is patience. How long will it take to get the phone working? There's a saying in Italy, which roughly translates to, "Never do today what can be put off till tomorrow." Everything slows down here. We have no car, so we walk everywhere. *Piano, piano!* (Slowly, slowly!)

We know this will be our primary residence for at least two, possibly four, years. We no longer have to pack up everything each time we leave; we keep clothes here when we travel to the States, and Bill leaves his painting supplies. For him this is a major relief; he doesn't have to ship his large unfinished paintings. There is a huge storage facility in the musty dungeon-like basement where he can store his canvases and paint supplies. He has adopted a process of renting a car and driving to the neighboring villages and sketching and working on small canvases. Then he returns to his studio, using them as a source for bigger paintings.

We want to play by the Italian set of rules. To order a *cappuccino* after lunch or dinner is a major violation of an Italian food rules. The Italians feel strongly that drinking milk after any meal will mess up the ability to digest food properly. Milk, which makes up over half of the contents of this drink, is considered a meal in itself, which is why people have it for breakfast. Never order cappuccino after 11 a.m. *"Due cappucci,"* I order with confidence; more casual than *cappuccino.* After 4 p.m., I switch from the salutation, *Buon giorno* to *buonasera* and like the locals often do, I just nod and say, "sera."

Because of the close proximity of other European cities, we travel from here—to St. Petersburg, Berlin, Paris and Vienna. We drive to the South of France (the most difficult part is getting out of Florence.) We make a big commitment to Florence and to each other. We return to the States in the summer and holidays to see our families and for art shows, and then come *home* to Florence.

We start taking the bus to Fiesole, the hilltop town of Etruscan origin, where we looked at the house, as a Sunday activity. The air is less polluted than in Florence and we liked to walk along Via di San Francesco, the steep path that leads to magnificent panoramic views of Florence and further up to the Monastery of San Francesco on the crest of the hill.

We wander about the Etruscan-Roman archeological area, which dates back to the 8th and 9th centuries, order a glass of wine at the tiny bar, and sit gazing in awe at the remains of the Roman theatre and baths.

This remarkable site really comes into its own during the annual "Slow Food" movement and wine tasting that takes place in Fiesole. Our friend Francesco lives here and much to the delight of my husband, there is an Irish pub, J.J. Hill, just as we step off the number 7 bus at Piazza Mino da Fiesole, the town's main square.

We start to emulate Florentine style – what the Italians call "sprezzatura," meaning a stylish nonchalance. Well-dressed Florentines are the norm. The women do not dash out to the market in sweats and running shoes, but are always elegant and smartly put together. I marvel at the elderly women, gray hair well-coiffed, dressed in flawless tweed suits and good looking walking shoes on their way to the market. Our mail is delivered by a gorgeous girl on a bicycle in her twenties, with long, thick, lustrous hair wearing skin-tight jeans, high heels, and a bright yellow vest with a sign on the back: *Poste Italiane.* No wonder my husband is forever checking our postbox. I vow to never again leave the house with wet hair or wearing sweatpants. I will focus on developing that put together Florentine look.

We live a few blocks from Supermercato Standa (now Conad) on Via Pietrapiana, a particularly filthy store, which sells basic supplies. It also sells meat and produce, but about a half a mile past there is Mercato di Sant'Ambrogio--a smaller and more manageable version of Mercato Centrale. Here is my favorite butcher, Macelleria Luca Menoni, and Scognamiglio for cheese and salumi. My favorite person at the butcher is Sandro, a handsome young flirtatious Florentine. I order in Italian: *un petto di pollo* (chicken breast), *uova fresche* (fresh eggs), *un mezzo kilo* (half a kilo) *manzo di macinata,* (ground beef) for sauce. He grinds it fresh and also corrects me in Italian when I make a mistake and he practices his English with me. "*Grazie,*" I say. "Thank you, Susan," replies my friend Sandro. Once I lied about what number I was holding after waiting over an hour for my holiday turkey and got caught, much to the delight of the surrounding Florentine women, who all started jabbering about me, but all I could understand was, "Americana." Then, I had to lug the thing home in my arms like an overweight newborn without a carriage.

We have many visitors who invariably say, "You must be fluent in Italian by now."

Actually, no, but I get by with my "tourist Italian." I can order out, shop at any market, and have intimate conversations as long as the person speaks slowly and enunciates every word while looking directly at me.

But this query usually elicits a defensive response in me because, God knows, I should be fluent by now. The justification I fall back to is the old "if you don't use it you lose it" cliché. I speak when I can here and have taken numerous classes. I lug the heavy language books back with me to the States when I leave, promising myself to study a minimum of one hour a day, but they remain unopened for eight months until I repacked them for the trip back. But now it will be different, I vow.

My husband returns to paint at his studio on Via de Tornabuoni, in the city center, and I continue to write and try to master Italian. In the past, when I would arrive at the language school for class each fall, they would ask, "Intermediate or advanced?" I would always rather be the smartest student in beginners than the stupidest in intermediate, especially as an older student. I would just keep repeating the novice level until it "clicked" and then move on. A 20-year-old can easily pick up a foreign language, but this is not the case for a mature woman who has always been left-brain-challenged. I sign up for an intensive class.

The truth is, you can live in this most tourist-thronged city and not speak a word of Italian. Most shopkeepers and restaurant workers speak some English. They often prefer Americans to speak English, so they can practice it. And almost invariably their English is better than the Italian of the American visitors, including mine.

The second most often-asked question is: "What do you do all day?" This is an easy one. On a typical day, we go for a walk around 9 a.m. and get a cappuccino at one of our favorite cafes. A good thing to know is if you stand at the bar the cost is generally 1.30 euro. The very same cup will be 6 euro if you choose to sit at a table and be waited on. The Italians generally stand at the bar and knock back the espresso or coffee quickly. Do you pay ahead for the coffee, or after? The split is about 50-50. Sometimes, you pay in advance and get a ticket, which you bring to the counter.

There is always a fabulous assortment of freshly baked brioche, some filled with jam, some with almond paste and some plain with perhaps a sprinkling of sugar. Our favorite spots are Caffè Rivoire in Piazza della Signoria, and La Loggia Degli Albizi, a few doors down from where we live; a lively café offering delectable pastries and a good lunch selection. But I think the best cappuccino in Florence can be found at the clothing designer, Roberto Cavalli's Caffè Giacosa on Via della Spada, on the corner of Via de' Tornabuoni. The steaming espresso with milk arrives in large cups with dark chocolate syrup swirled on top of the foam. Mostly local business people frequent here.

After this treasured jolt, we may walk to the bank ATM for cash or possibly to the post office to wait in line for a stamp to mail a letter in the fervent hope that it will arrive at the intended destination. The Italian mails are notoriously unreliable. Bill then goes to his studio to paint and I may walk to the Mercato di Sant'Ambrogio for cheese and prosciutto and bread for lunch, then on to my laptop to write. Before we know it, the day is almost over and we finish up at 5 or 6.

Since Bill's studio is several streets from our home, we usually meet for an *aperitivo* in Piazza della Signoria, centrally located between the studio and our apartment. The *aperitivo* is a civilized custom, when people meet all over Florence in pubs and bars to relax with an end of the day drink. This usually takes place between 5:30 and 7:30 p.m. Typically, there is an appetizer buffet set up, along with plates so that you can help yourself to the tasty treats such as mini sandwiches and pizzas, nuts and olives. It can be pricey or not depending on the establishment and part of town. Across the Ponte Vecchio (Oltrarno), or as Mary McCarthy, the author, describes it, "the Left Bank of Florence," the drinks are usually more economical. One of our favorite spots there is Enoteca Le volpi e l'uva. (The fox and the grape, from the Aesop fable), in Piazza dei Rossi.

Some say the custom started for digestive purposes. Italians believe a drink like Campari and soda "opens the stomach." If you launch into your three-course meal without first awakening the digestive tract with an *aperitivo*, you're just asking for problems. I'm sure a glass of wine has the same effect. While we sip our evening drink, we decide on where to have dinner.

There are many great restaurants in Florence and in our earlier years, as part-time residents and new to the city, we sampled quite a few of them. Now, as permanent residents, we've whittled the list down to a few, which we consider our extended dining room. Over the years these have provided us with clear insights into the real-world lives of Florentines. Many of these people have become our friends over the last decade, as we have watched their families grow and prosper. For example, when two brothers, Luciano and Donatello, were young single waiters at Buca Poldo on via Chiasso degli Armagnati, working for our friend and then-owner, Franco, we got to know and like them. Now they are the owners, they are both married with children, and we have a celebration dinner with the entire family every year. Several of Bill's paintings hang in the restaurant.

Our other favorite trattoria is Cammillo, in Oltrarno district on Borgo S. Jacopo, which serves the most authentic classic Florentine food in a rustic, bustling setting. The quality of steaks and veal chops are superb, and the white Tuscan beans and fresh pasta are the best in the city.

If you have only one opportunity to dine in Florence, this would be my recommendation. The clients are a mix of noble Italian families amidst tourists. It was Ferdinando and Rosaria Frescobaldi who first told us about Cammillo.

As you enter the front door, there is an appetizer and dessert workspace immediately on the left, behind glass in front of a seven-foot-high antique credenza. Next is a young woman sitting in a wooden booth, collecting money from the waiters and calculating their bills. There is a private room upstairs that seats 24.

The waiters are all superb, but our favorite is Arturo. We always request his table and sit in the front room, where we have a full view of the kitchen. The professional servers stand at attention, wearing starched white shirts, black bowties, and slacks with white aprons rolled at the waist. As the door opens Chiara greets each guest personally while referring to a reservation list. Bill calls the dining experience at Cammillo an opera, which starts around 8 p.m., when the flow of diners enter and the kitchen and waiters come to life. The waiters scurry about with the *primo* course, the wine, and the water. If we are with a group, we are likely to have been lucky enough to sit at the big square "family table" right next to the wide-open kitchen—a step down from the front dining room. We stay the full evening and are never rushed.

Chiara Massiero is a tall, gracious woman who is the third generation of her family to oversee Cammillo since it opened in 1945. Her mother's father was the original owner. She and her handsome husband Massimo have become friends and have been to our home in Florence. Bill has several paintings hanging here among the diverse collection of artwork covering the walls of this unreconstructed Florentine trattoria.

In the autumn of 2004, we are invited to the Ugolino Golf Club for Thanksgiving. This course, founded in 1889 by the British colony in Florence, is the first golfing association in Italy. A short ride from Florence by car, it is located in Impruneta, essentially a suburb of Florence.

The American consulate greeted about one hundred of us expatriates, and a gorgeous turkey dinner was served, complete with warm apple pie for dessert. The views of the golf course, with its cypress and olive trees, are spectacular. Bill was mesmerized, never having seen a golf course with olive trees. He took his camera outside to capture the views, which he would paint.

By December I have completed four weeks of school, five days a week, four hours a day; I receive a *certificato,* saying that I have completed 80 hours of lessons. My head is swirling with verb tenses, vocabulary, and colloquialisms.

We stay through Christmas and New Year's for the first time and attend a Christmas Eve concert at Teatro Verdi, a popular 160-year-old theater in the city center on Via Ghibellini, close to Piazza Santa Croce. We leave the theater and head into the frosty night air and on to Midnight Mass at the Duomo, where Dominican monks sing Gregorian chants. It is magical. Bill has filled a flask with Irish whiskey and slipped it in his coat pocket; he takes a few nips along the way. On New Year's Eve we are invited to a party at a friend's condo even though they are in California. Suzanne, our rental agent, says they have agreed in their absence to let a "few friends" celebrate at her magnificent apartment with a grand terrace along the Arno. "Oh, one more thing," Suzanne says, "Don't forget to wear your red underwear to ring in the New Year! They say it'll bring you luck."

I walk in the blustery cold to Intimissimi on Via dei Calzaiuoli. This is the co-ed version of Victoria's Secret in Italy. I find the perfect pair of red boxer shorts for Bill, who cannot wait to drop his pants and show them off as the hour strikes midnight.

We arrive to find a festive atmosphere, with an international mix of about a hundred people—Italians, Americans and Australians, along with a 3-piece band. Although the musicians sing the English lyrics to the rock 'n' roll songs, they don't exactly speak English. I tell Suzanne that Bill does a routine where he plays the air guitar and sings Chuck Berry's "Johnny B. Goode."

Always enthusiastic, she tells the band that we have a singer who would like to perform. Bill says I am the instigator. So I talk to the band but am unable to translate the word for broom. Suzanne locates one in the kitchen. I assure them that they won't regret it–"*Non ve ne pentirete*"—and up Bill steps to the low platform, with no persuasion at all, for an absolutely rollicking rendition that brings the house down.

The party comes alive, the band members are deliriously happy, and everyone is dancing. But then he won't leave and, huddling with the band, the guitarist announces that Bill Kelley, *"ora cantare,"* will now sing the Creedence Clearwater Revival rendition of "Proud Mary." The revelers who are all dancing go wild. Guests want to know where Bill will be performing next and Suzanne suggests that he might give up painting and devote himself fully to playing the broom and singing with the band.

Laura and Portis leave well before midnight with a warning: "Keep an eye out for falling objects if you're walking around near midnight!" Sometime after midnight, we leave the party and join the hordes of people moving as one mass down the streets as we attempt to walk home amid exploding fireworks and broken glass. We are witness to a strange tradition in Florence. People throw bottles and all kinds of stuff out the windows. Debris is everywhere.

There is an old custom that is still followed in some places of throwing your old things out the window to symbolize your readiness to accept the New Year. On New Year's Day, we welcome 2005 with a homemade Italian dinner with our Florentine friend Adrianna and her husband, Shelby.

It's Laura's idea to give cooking classes to our husbands as a Christmas gift. She figures Portis would never go alone, so if Bill goes with him, it will cement the deal. Indeed it does. She has done the research and decides on Trattoria Garga. The culinary class will involve cooking Tuscan fare in a 16th-century palazzo right in the heart of Florence. They promise "an experience to remember and cherish, with a maximum of twelve participants."

The day arrives and it is like watching your children go off to school. Portis and Bill are wound up and energized as they make their departure in late morning. "If you think the women love me now, wait till they find out I can cook," Bill says.

In the evening they return in a more subdued state. We query them about every aspect but the answers are brief. When Bill and I are alone, I ask him what's wrong and if he didn't enjoy the class. "How did you two possibly find an all-lesbian class to send us to?" he says. "It was me, Portis, and ten gay women." I cannot stop laughing.

In April, we go to New York for Bill's art show at The Walter Wickiser gallery in Soho. The gallery had produced a book of his paintings featuring quotes from Sister Wendy Beckett, the respected BBC and PBS art historian. She has become a big fan of Bill's paintings, even calling him, "The spiritual son to Cezanne."

When we return from our successful exhibition in New York, time is running out at the Tournabuoni studio. The two-year lease will be up in June and the Maestro has to find new space. We decide to look for a small property to buy in Florence, despite the admonitions of friends who advise against it. Corso finds a good space for sale in the Santo Spirito Quarter, the (other side of the Arno River), a part of Florence that still belongs to the Florentines. The asking price is 230,000 euro for what would be studio space of only 550 sq. feet. Corso says it is overpriced and suggests we offer 200,000. We make the offer and they turn it down, and that is the end of that deal. They do not do a lot of negotiation of prices in Italy, unlike in America.

And then Bill finds the perfect studio space for rent on the Ponte Vecchio, the oldest bridge in Italy, on the corner of San Jacopo, Oltrarno. Here, on the top floor, overlooking the Arno River with four massive windows and perfect light, Bill will paint in ideal surroundings. He signs the same annual agreement we have for our apartment, two years with possible two-year extension.

Florence is a walking city, with cobblestone streets and rocky sidewalks. I wear my pedometer on my right hip pocket and clock my steps—mostly in flat shoes. Occasionally, for an event, I branch out into low heels, no higher than two and one-quarter inches.

One evening, on my way to Lisa's house for a dinner party, I round the corner of Via Dante Alighieri and step with my right foot into a gap directly in front of the courthouse, *Commune di Firenze*, on Via dei Maggazzini. Piazza San Martino is among the worst areas in the city, loaded with potholes and loose stones. I twist my ankle and knee. It is an unlikely place for such an obvious disaster waiting to happen. I promise myself that in the future I will wear more sensible shoes.

Lisa introduces us to Gina and Ed, her neighbors in New York who have come to Florence so their captivating eight-year-old son can attend the International School, formerly known as The American School of Florence, which was founded by Horace Gibson, who is another of Lisa's great friends. They wanted the Italian experience and their son was young enough so they could still move around before school became too serious. In September we get together with Ed and Lisa for dinner at Trattoria Carmine. Suzanne has been showing Ed villas to lease. We're struck by how much Ed sounds like Steven Van Zandt in *The Sopronos.*

Ed and Gina move into an elaborate palazzo in Santo Spirito, owned by a member of the Frescobaldi family. It is the perfect venue for entertaining, with the bonus of a huge back yard so all the kids can play outside. Because of them, and all the lavish parties they give in their magnificent villa, we meet our friends Mary and Mario, and numerous other Florentines. Our circle of friends grows and grows.

The Lady Garden

Following a summer visit with children and grandchildren in the States, we return in August of 2005 to our beautiful home on Borgo degli Albizi. Bill takes possession of his newly leased studio on the Ponte Vecchio. In no time, we are back in our routine. Corso invites Bill to play at Ugolino Golf Club. He is a member *and* he has a car. Bill gets the idea to paint the first hole of the course and he starts a 6x7-foot canvas in his new studio. He decides to take one day off a week from painting to play golf with Ed. "Fridays with Eddie," he calls it, and that is about the only reason he takes a day off from painting in his studio.

My personal Florentine schedule includes writing, Italian class, and some form of exercise. My previous experience with Keith at the Florence Dance Center was mostly a stretching and toning class. It was very convenient when I lived on the other side of the Arno River. This fall, I decide to join an actual health club, where I can use the machines, treadmill, and bikes. No one speaks English but I am familiar with the equipment from using them at the gym in Florida. There will be no surprises, or so I think. I can walk the few blocks past the Duomo in my sneakers and gym clothes, so I do not have to change, but I do need to put my pocketbook and jacket in a locker in the women's dressing area.

The first time I walk into the room of naked women I am in shock. After showering, they stand around chatting and spending what seems like an inordinate amount of time rubbing cream lavishly on their perfectly toned bodies and flawless skin. Not one of them looks like they need to exercise. The European women are more comfortable with their bodies than Americans. I can't help noticing that many of the women have designs carved in their pubic hair; a topiary in what the English call "the lady garden." Some have initials, others variations of a Mohawk design, several completely shaved and one, a heart. Then there was the assortment of uncomfortable-looking thong undies. How could I *not* stare at such a display? Growing up as the only girl with five brothers in a Catholic family, there was not a great deal of nudity in my household; in fact, there was none.

One day, having nagged Bill for weeks, I come to the realization that he is not going to change the hallway light bulb. I carry the ladder to the spot, position it, and climb up to do the task. I have to put on reading glasses, so I can see the tiny screws that need to be removed before I can reach the bulb. As I descend, still wearing the disorienting magnifiers, I miss the step, spin off the ladder, and land on the sharp corner of a nearby table that was holding a stereo and about 100 CDs. The crash brings Bill running, who finds me lying on the floor covered in boxed disks. I have sharp pains in my back and think I've probably cracked a few ribs. I call the English-speaking doctor, who sends me back to Istituto Fanfani for an X-ray.

After waiting on line for a few hours, I explain my problem: *"Ho bisogno di un X-ray delle mie costole,"* and follow a woman into the room where I lie on a table as directed while the technician performs her task. The next day, I return for the results. *"No, non è scoleosis. La spina dorsale è in buone condizioni."*

The good news is that I don't have scoliosis. But then I never thought I did. The bad news is that they have X-rayed the wrong body part. I locate an orthopedic doctor who informs me that it doesn't really matter, because there is no treatment for cracked ribs anyway, they just have to heal on their own. He will do an X-ray if I insist, asking, *"Come male avete bisogno di sapere se si è rotto le costole?"* (How badly do you need to know if you cracked your ribs?) There's a saying among Americans in Florence, "Where do you go if you need medical help?" Answer: "The airport."

When I start feeling better, we take a train trip to Milan that includes a pilgrimage to Leonardo da Vinci's painting, *Il Cenacolo* (*The Last Supper*), located inside the Refectory at the Monastery of Santa Maria delle Grazie in central Milan. We read the tickets are hard to come by, so Bill books in advance. The painting, which measures 180 inches x 350 inches, is a mural, not a fresco, as it was painted on a dry wall and not on wet plaster. Because of the method and materials used by Leonardo, the painting is very fragile. Finished in 1498, it covers the back wall of the convent's dining hall. We are fortunate to have the opportunity to spend 15 minutes of relative solitude in front of one of the world's greatest works of art.

We take a small group tour of La Scala, the world-renowned opera house, and sneak off in the middle, without anyone noticing. Like children, we try all the private doors leading to the box seats and find one unlocked. We slink in and are fortunate to catch a dress rehearsal in progress. "Wouldn't it be amazing to make love right here?" Bill whispers. "Yeah, I can see the headlines; middle-aged American couple arrested in Italy for lewd and lascivious activity at the opera," I reply. "Would a *pompino* be out of the question?" he asks.

A security official catches us as we make our escape from the box. He asks where we came from and what we were doing there unescorted. We do our best absent-minded American routine until he finally escorts us out.

———— ∞∞ ————

Bill is asked to donate, in exchange for golf privileges at the club, his now complete giant 6x7-foot landscape of the first hole at Ugolino. Having a painting accepted by the oldest, most prestigious golf course in Italy is a big deal. It has to be voted on and accepted by the board. Not only is Bill not a Florentine, he isn't even Italian. It is unanimously accepted. Now we have to find a framer who will build the massive frame. Our older international artist friend, Freddie Fuchs, recommends Casa della Cornice on Via Pietro Toselli, which houses the largest assortment of frames I have ever seen. Here they will custom-build a frame specific for the painting. When complete, they bring it to the studio by truck, attach it, and deliver it to the club with Bill and Corso following in their car. We gather with a few friends at the end of November to celebrate the installation. It hangs in the club today, a singular honor for an American artist and has led to numerous painting sales.

An annual event that takes place in Florence, just a few blocks from where we live, is the *Scoppio del Carro*, or the "Explosion of the Cart", which dates back over 350 years. An elaborate wagon built in 1622 and standing two to three stories high is pulled by a pair of oxen decorated in garlands through the streets of Florence to the square between the Baptistry and Cathedral. We are in a competition with our neighbors, Laura and Portis, to see which of us will get a better view of the spectacle.

The cart, properly rigged with a suitable arsenal of fireworks, then sits in front of the cathedral. From the altar, at around 11 a.m., when the "Gloria" is sung inside the church, the Archbishop uses the fire to light a dove–shaped rocket (called the "*colombina*" and symbolizing the Holy Spirit), and this in turns flies out down a wire to the outside of the church and collides with the Cart in the square, setting off a spectacular firework display to the cheers of all.

If the complicated ritual proceeds smoothly and all of the fireworks go off, good luck is ensured for a good harvest for this year as well as for the city and its citizens—so we hope for a wonderful explosion of the cart every Easter. The explosion in the year 2006 went off without a hitch, heralding for us a series of extraordinary events.

———∞∞∞———

Bill has a "starving artist" friend about forty years old, Dejan Bogdanovic, who arrived in Florence from the former Yugoslavia on a SACI (Studio Art Centers International) scholarship in the early '90s. SACI, the oldest American art school in Florence, is a U.S. non-profit university-level school for undergraduate and graduate students seeking fully accredited studio art, design, and liberal arts instruction. After Dejan graduated, he stayed in Florence, as so many artists do, but he found it difficult to support himself on the sales of his paintings. So he sustains his passion by working as a waiter at The Golden View, a popular restaurant. This is where we first met him at dinner one evening and a conversation about art and painting ensued. Bill and Dejan became friends and decided to share the studio on Via Tournbuoni. They worked well together, as his work is, dark and brooding, as opposed to Bill's outrageously colorful landscapes. During this time, Dejan, tall and slender with a shock of brunette hair, met a beautiful young woman, Anina Stancu, a prima ballerina with the Berlin Ballet company. Whenever she comes to Florence, we try to get together with this charming couple.

Anina gives me a travel book about Montenegro and says they want to plan a two-week trip with us next May to Croatia, Dubrovnik, and Montenegro, where the beaches are beautiful. Bill thinks this is a fabulous idea, as this is Dejan's homeland and it will be great to travel with natives. I have no desire to get into a bathing suit next to a 27-year-old ballerina. I'll have to find one with sleeves and a full skirt. Many things can change by next May, but not my mind. I don't want to go. I hope Bill will forget.

For the moment, we decide on what turns out to be a carefree car trip to the enchanting village of Bolgheri and the seaside town of San Lorenzo. This is a gorgeous wine-producing area, unspoiled by tourism, located about an hour and three-quarters drive from Florence. Dejan has rented a car and made reservations at a hotel as well as at the No. 1 rated restaurant in Italy at the time, Gamberi Rossi, a tiny eatery by the sea. We have a delectable meal accompanied by the excellent local wines, Vermentino Bolgheri and the famous red, Sassicaia. The trip provides many new painting opportunities for Bill and Dejan. After returning from Bolgheri, we now embark on a trip of a lifetime, from Florence to China.

In early May, we take off on a full KLM 747 flight, from Rome to Beijing for our five week trip to

China, which begins at the Peninsula Palace Hotel. Bill has read the *Eyewitness Guide to China* from cover to cover and is excited for us to see this country together. On our second day, we meet up with our wonderful, knowledgeable guide and translator, Amanda Yang, and a driver, Mr. Tu, who take us the short distance to the Forbidden City. That's the policy here, a guide *and* a driver. As we enter China's most popular single-site tourist attraction, through the entrance in Tiananmen Square, we are disappointed by what first catches our eye, a Starbucks. The Forbidden City itself transported us back centuries to Imperial China and was unforgettable.

Our guide Amanda soon starts calling Bill the "Professor," because when she asks us a question pertaining to the history of Beijing, he always knows the answer. "The Professor is never wrong." She asks, "How much older are you than Susan, Professor?" He says "a couple of years." "Oh, you look much older." As we stand at the palace inside the Forbidden City, she explains about concubines. Bill smiles and wants to know more. "The professor can only dream about concubines," our guide says. Bill observes that the Chinese consider slurping, spitting, and belching in public quite acceptable. "Hey, they make me look good," he says. After a long day of sightseeing and lectures, we return to the hotel to change before Amanda and Mr. Tu once again pick us up and take us to Courtyard 7 restaurant for a delectable dinner of Peking duck, which would be our best meal in China.

It's not the familiar American Chinese food we find in China; no chicken with cashews or sweet and sour shrimp. Rather, it is bulls' testicles, eel, squirrel, turtle, and even cat and dog; a good place for a diet, I decide.

We take a trip to The Great Wall at Mutianyu. We learn that the elephant is the sign of universal peace. So why are the Chinese responsible for so much elephant slaughter just so trinkets can be carved from elephants' tusks?

In Nanjing, we will learn that the lion is the symbol of power and that 8 is the lucky and prosperous number. We learn about the one-child rule in this country. But if the first child is a girl or handicapped, you may have one more.

The day we board the ship for the rest of our journey I am able to check emails. I have a response from an agent who has agreed to take on my manuscript, *Time to Say Goodbye*, the novel about my father.

Our real estate hassles follow us even to China, and we have to deal with another housing crisis. The two-year lease on our Florence apartment is expiring. With limited email access on the ship, I have a message from our neighbor Laura that the realtor has brought some people who are looking to rent our condo. We have it until September 1, and it is only May. Somehow we have to call the owners to tell them we are definitely extending. According to our rental contract in Florence, we pay the real estate agent a commission for the first two years. After that, we can negotiate directly with the owners.

We try to call the owners and let them know we are taking it and to please relate this to the agent. It is no easy task, calling Italy from a ship cruising down the Yangtze River, but, with the assistance of the ship's technical people, we manage to get through. On June 1, our second to last day before docking in Hong Kong, I get an email from the new agent that my manuscript is being read by a potential publisher. At night there is karaoke after dinner and Bill brings the place to its feet with his sing-along rendition of "Johnny B Goode." He's becoming an international performer.

After an exhausting and exhilarating trip, we return home to Florence and settle back into our routine. We sign a new two-year annual contract on our home, as well as one on the Bill's studio. Bill is eager to start painting scenes from China. He says what he saw there changed his style; his colors become stronger and brighter. Back in his studio, he starts to paint his version of the Great Wall of China in Tuscan colors.

Trattoria Antellesi, a historic venue in the center of the city located inside a 15th-century building, in the shadow of Mercato Centrale on Via Faenza, is one of our favorite spots for dinner. Shortly after our return to Florence, Franco and Rosa, the owners, invite us to their daughter's *cresima,* confirmation. We have become family as we watched their children grow up.

We arrive at Palazzo Borghese for the after party; it is an historic building dating back to 1437, now used for receptions, conferences, and events. Their son, Frederico, has a small band, which is entertaining the crowd. To our utter amazement, they are playing Irish music and all the kids are dancing and singing along to "The Wild Colonial Boy." We are seated with the family, who couldn't be more delighted that Maestro Kelley (from Boston) knows every lyric to every song.

One night in June, strolling home from our 17th anniversary dinner, we are stopped by four American teenage girls, who ask if we would take a picture of them with their camera. "Sure, happy to." My husband asks where they were from.

"North Carolina"—they are studying in Firenze. "Art history," says one. So Bill, under the influence and glow of several glasses of Chianti says, "I'm a famous painter, perhaps you've heard of me." Well, indeed they had not and politely turned to me. "How about you, do you pose for him?" one girl asks. "No, I write." "Oh," she says, bored, looking off in the direction of the gelato place they were headed. "What do you write?"

"Relationship books—like, *Why Men Commit*." Everyone, of any age, is always interested in relationships. One girl perks up. "They don't commit," she states flatly. "Oh, but most of them do eventually," I tell her. The other girl says, "I think I saw you on *Oprah*. Were you on *Oprah*?" I say, "Yes, but that was a while ago." "I saw you, too," the second girl says, her voice now a high squeak. She turns to Bill and hands him her camera. "Will you take our picture with your wife? This is so exciting."

Bill complies, despite his disappointment that these young women are more into commitment issues than art. They head off, chattering and giggling, toward their gelato.

Bill rolls his eyes. "You know," he tells me as we walk away, "when you were on *Oprah*, these girls would have been around seven years old."

One of the great annual summer events in Florence takes place at the end of June. *La Festa di San Giovanni*—The Feast of St John—is an annual public holiday for the patron saint of Florence. Celebrations run through the day. During the morning, there's a flag bearer's procession and a parade in Renaissance costumes. In the afternoon, attendees split their time between the traditional rowing race on the Arno and Florentine kick game *calcio storico,* (also known as "historic football"), an early form of football that originated in 16th-century Italy. Florentine kick game matches take place in Piazza Santa Croce.

We have been invited by some of our Florentine friends to the Florence Rowing Club, *Società Canottieri,* a unique private venue located just below the Uffizi Gallery, along the Arno River. Round tables have been set up on the grass and a stunning three-course dinner is served by formally attired waiters. We are in place for a perfect view of the most awaited moment of the day, when the Patron Saint of Florence is honored by a beautiful display —the *fochi* fireworks at 10:00 pm fired from Piazzale Michelangelo. This is our final summer event before our return to the states to our visit with our families.

Sister Wendy Beckett

The relationship between Bill and Sister Wendy Beckett began in May 2002, when she sent a note to the Walter Wickiser Gallery in New York, where he was having a solo exhibition. She had seen a photo of his painting, *Tranquillo*, a large, 5x6-foot colorful landscape of the Chianti region in *ARTnews,* the oldest and most widely circulated art magazine in the world, read by collectors, dealers, historians, artists, museum directors, and curators. She expressed an interest in "seeing more of the work of William Kelley. It seems to have a lyrical strength which is quite moving." And thus the friendship was born. To this day, he often sends her photos of his new paintings. She responds with her comments and has written glowingly about them.

The so-called "Art Nun," Sister Wendy is arguably the best-known, most beloved art historian in the world. Following her childhood vocation, she joined the Sisters of Notre Dame at 16 and graduated from Oxford with highest honors in 1953. She went on to live and teach in South Africa and even served for a time as a Reverend Mother. She returned to England in 1970 to live a fully contemplative life in a hermitage on the grounds of the Carmelite monastery at Quidenham, Norfolk, England. She leaves the hermitage only when necessary to make her television shows. She continues to live there, spending the majority of each day in prayer, silence, and solitude.

Reluctantly, she entered the public arena in 1991, appearing on BBC television in a documentary on the National Gallery, London. Popular acclaim brought her back to television as the commentator for *Sister Wendy's Odyssey*, six short films about art treasures around Great Britain, and *Sister Wendy's Grand Tour*, a series on European art. In 1997, *Sister Wendy's Story of Painting* expanded her enthusiastic following to include American audiences. Her most recent series, *Sister Wendy's American Collection* (2001) takes viewers on a tour of six American museums.

She leaves seclusion infrequently and only for art-related visits to "particular art" she has chosen to see. In November 2006, she was going to the Vatican to complete an audiotape about the Sistine Chapel before continuing on to the Basilica of San Domenico in Bologna. After months of barely legible notes and postcards expressing her desire to come to Florence, she puts us in touch with a priest, Father Steve Blair, who is in charge of her travel planning, and gives us his email address.

Father Steve writes back that although he doesn't know who William Kelley is, Sister Wendy insists on coming to his studio and meeting him. I write back inviting them to stay with us.

The next morning, I open my e-mail and read with delight:

Dear William and Susan,

Thank you for your kind offer to visit on 15 Nov and to spend the night. We'd be very happy to accept if it wouldn't be too much of an inconvenience. It conjures up images of E.M. Forester's *A Room With a View*...it's very generous of you to invite us.

By way of introductions (so you know what you're in for), you of course have seen Sr. Wendy through her programs and I can only say that she is just as delightful in person...a very warm, caring and affectionate woman. I've often felt so fortunate to be able to travel with her on occasion and to benefit from the wealth of her knowledge, experience and faith.

I think I told you a little about myself, but to re-cap...I'm an Air Force Chaplain/Priest whose home is in the UK not too far from the Monastery where Sr. Wendy lives. I belong to the UK Diocese of East Anglia. I met Sr. Wendy about 7 years ago and we've become good friends since then. The other person who makes up our traveling trio is Rod Stephens, who lives in Irvine, California. Rod and I went to the seminary together and have been good friends for the last 40 years. His work is in art and design of liturgical and sacred space.

Looking forward to meeting up with you, until then, best wishes,
Cheers,
Steve

Two months pass and the "pastoral visitation" is upon us. I go into meal-planning mode. Will they be here for lunch, tea, dinner? Do they have special dietary needs? Does she go to restaurants? I walk to Bar Vivoli near Sante Croce, renowned for their homemade gelato and homemade pastry, and order a ricotta, egg, and tomato quiche and cookies.

What do they drink? Bill tells me to buy a bottle of Scotch; "All priests drink Scotch. And get a bottle of white wine for the studio." What do they eat for breakfast? I do a last-minute check of their accommodations: I fluff pillows, and put a vase of fresh flowers, bottled water and glasses, chocolates, and fresh towels in their rooms.

I make a trip to San Lorenzo market to buy pecorino cheese, fruit, crackers, and salami. I think we are ready, but truly have no idea what to expect. Bill is excited she will see his newest work, which includes some paintings from our recent trip to China, and hopes she likes it.

We are meeting David, our friend and driver, in Piazza della Republica at 2:45. They are arriving at the train station at 3:24. We know what Sister Wendy looks like and we know they have a portable wheelchair.

I see them first, behind a pillar. "Hi," I say. "You're an easy group to spot." She takes my hand, kisses me, and smiles her signature toothy smile. Fathers Rod and Steve I like immediately. I can sense their goodness and genuine fondness for this woman they are looking after. "Oh, yes," she says holding my hand, "you can't miss us, two handsome men and a woman in black."

We arrive at the waiting van and the two priests pull her up from the chair. "It's a miracle I can walk," she says, with a gleeful smile. I go to pick up her small travel case and remark on how heavy it is. "Oh, it's just Sister's cosmetics and jewelry," says Father Rod. They're funny! How often do you meet someone and find they immediately feel like family—good family? My husband has admonished me to not pull out my camera immediately and start snapping photos. But Father Rod beats me to it and starts shooting photos the moment he is off the train with his Casio digital. Rod is 58, Steve is 59, and Sister Wendy describes herself as a "very old 76 with some health problems." She has disk problems in her neck, causing limited mobility. Her heart is weak.

We pile into the van and we ask if they prefer to go to our apartment and settle in or go directly to Bill's studio. "Oh, to the studio," says Sister Wendy. "Definitely, the studio first."

The streets in Florence are impossibly narrow and one-way, so back and forth we go until we arrive at the corner of Borgo San Jacopo and the Ponte Vecchio—not only the oldest bridge in the city, but the only one that escaped being blown up in World War II. Today, it is lined on both sides with jewelry shops and is a tourist magnet in the heart of Florence. Bill's studio, at Number 2 Ponte Vecchio (Oltrarno), is located on the fifth floor of a medieval building and has a magnificent view of the Duomo.

The elevator only holds two, so Sister Wendy and Bill get in and the two priests and I walk the five flights of stairs. Bill opens the door and turns on the light. His huge (6x7-foot) canvas of the Great Wall of China dominates the room. "I love it," Sister Wendy says. "It's extraordinary."

She and Bill are drawn to each other in a mystical way, and, in fact they share a birthday, February 25. My husband tells her it was also his father's birthday. "We have an eighth century English saint whose name date is February 25th," she says. "She's the patron saint of ulcers and rabies. I was hoping for something a little more romantic than ulcers and rabies, but at least we have a patron saint." We are all laughing, and she turns to Bill. "If a mad dog bites you, you're all set."

I offer her a glass of water, and she asks for a glass of wine. I am glad I have the white wine Bill had suggested.

She walks around the small studio holding my husband's hand, telling him how much she loves all the work and particularly his Tuscan landscapes, including several from Ugolino golf course outside of Florence. "The few times I've seen TV, I've watched sports. I don't like tennis, because I don't like confrontation," she says. I like to watch golf and snooker. I love to watch Ernie Els, he's so graceful." She asks Bill about golf and he tells her he tries to plays once a week at the club.

She looks at each painting with great care and tells Father Rod to take photos of all of them. "Incredible paintings," she says. "No duds here." Bill has a series of three grape paintings that he has just completed. After careful study, she describes individually the mood of each grape painting as, "serene, passionate, and dreamy." She asks which one is my favorite. I point to the "dreamy" one.

A friend had just told me that our new digital camera, recently purchased and never used, takes short video clips. I try my hand and manage to get a few brief movies of Sister Wendy and Bill. My favorite part of the video is when she faces the camera, head on, and says, "It's so wonderful to have Susan so completely entered into your vision. You need her," using her expressive hands, with a twinkle in her eyes.

She admits she would welcome an "end to these wretched excursions from contemplative life," but the media requests are still streaming in. "Somehow my very ordinary persona, my plain face, and my obvious love for what I am talking about has drawn people in. As long as I have the physical strength I will continue."

She had just stayed at the Hotel Hassler in Rome and had been asked to be photographed with Tom Cruise. She declined, but was curious about him. Because she's been on TV promoting her books she tells us that one newscaster asked her to review *The Devil Wears Prada*. Once again, she politely declined.

"You see, Susan," she says over a cup of tea later that day, "My life is very simple. I wear the same thing every day, and I eat the same food, leftover vegetables, every day. This frees all my time for prayer and creativity." She explains that she owns two habits, and she is wearing the "good one," which has many darned patches. Her charm, keen wit, and sharp mind are ever present. Her pockets are like two saddlebags from which she removes the contents and carefully places them on our kitchen table: A tiny wooden icon that opens to reveal three images of the Madonna; a larger religious painting on wood; a tiny Buddha in a case from Tibet. "I can get through security without a problem because my pockets are deep," she says, although nothing she has shown us would set off an alarm.

Later, she sits in our bedroom, looking at the frescoes on the walls and drinking a glass of wine. She, Father Steve and Father Rod stay with us overnight.

"She doesn't miss a trick," Father Steve says. Oh, yes, and she has very definite opinions and does not back down. She knows who she is and what she wants. The following morning at the Duomo, she says to Father Rod, "I want you to tip the wheelchair, so I can see the frescoes on the ceiling." "Yes, dear," he responds, and she laughs.

After spending Christmas in Boston with family, we return to Florence in the New Year.

I begin working on an updated version of my formerly best-selling *Why Men Commit* book at the request of the publishing company, Adams Media. When I finally complete the proposal and send it off, I find out that the editor has left the company and am directed to his replacement, a recent college graduate who asks me, "Why would you think we would be interested in a book that is fifteen years old?" "Because the editor was checking best-selling numbers on past titles and he called me and requested I do the proposal," I say. She seems perplexed, and that is the end of all the hard work I had put into the project. I set it aside and return to work on a story for *Sarasota Magazine* about Sister Wendy's visit to Florence.

I begin to plan our trip to Russia. Because so many of our trips revolve around art, we are really looking forward to seeing The State Hermitage Museum in St. Petersburg, which has one of the largest collections of Western European art in the world. But we need to get visas, and this brings me to the reason we should all keep the economy moving and use a visa service as we did for China. I did not take into consideration that we would be dealing with both the Italian and the Russian bureaucracy if we did it on our own. I don't feel comfortable leaving our passports in the care of unknown travel agents. One website says the Russian consulate in Rome has morning and afternoon hours. They also say we should get a visa voucher by applying on the web, which I do ($45 x 2=$90). It is not possible to reach them by phone as I call every day and the line is always busy. We take the morning train (66 euro x 2) and arrive in Rome in a torrential storm, hail a taxi (20 euro) and arrive at the consulate on Via Nomentana at 11:35. The security guard points to a rather large sign that says 8-11:30 am Monday-Thursday. It is Wednesday and the door is slammed in our face. It is still pouring and the streets are now flooded, so as we stand on the curb trying to get a taxi (10 euro), cars drive through puddles and splash us with dirty water—one getting me all over my face and hair. I want to cry. We are now soaked and we have the choice of trying to find a place to stay and returning tomorrow morning at 8, or taking the train back to Florence. We go to the American Express office. They tell us it will take 10 working days to get a visa. We decide to stay over and book a hotel (230 euro), right off the Via Veneto, and we walk to the Pantheon and have lunch (46 euro). We drink wine; we have to. We attempt to change our return train tickets (66 euro) for the next day but the rain has caused the lines to be out. They tell us we can change them tomorrow for a slight fee. We walk around all day, buy toothbrushes and toothpaste (12 euro) and T-shirts to sleep in (10 euro), underwear (12.50 euro) and some facial cleanser and eye cream (28 euro). Bill buys disposable razors so they will let him in the consulate the next morning (8 euro). We find a lovely outdoor spot, Alex Café, for dinner, as the rain has ceased (87.50 euro).

The next day we return by taxi to the consulate at 8:10 a.m. (10 euro). We wait about an hour with all of our documents and photos and unnecessary pre-visa voucher and mandatory invitation from Russian hotel. We are finally let into a big room with one man who does not speak English *or* Italian, and he inspects our documents with great care and stamps them. He then directs us to the cashier: 250 euro per person for same day service; they don't mail the visas. I notice, gathered around a big table, no fewer than 13 service people getting visas for all kinds of tours and cruises. Then there are about 8 people like us, doing it themselves. Bill is very annoyed as he approaches the pay window with his *credito* card, all the while mumbling "scam."

"No," the woman says, "cash only." I had brought along a check book. Again she says, "No, cash only."

Bill has to leave the consulate, where he is directed to an ATM machine that is going to spit out 500 euro (we have found most have limits of 250 euro). He leaves without his blue "visitors pass" and I begin to wonder if they will let him back in and if I will ever see him again. He returns in 20 minutes, hand full of paper bills, smiling. I ask him why he is smiling. He says, "Because there is a long line outside of the consulate and I just walked to the front of the line to get back in." Three hours pass and we finally get the visas. Thanks to the combination of Russians and Italians, let's just say that no one was in a hurry. We take a taxi to the train (10 euro) and try to change our ticket. The guy says it is no good because we didn't change the day before. We try to explain that the lines were down but he just says, "No." So we buy new first-class tickets back to Florence (94 euro); coach was sold out. Bottom line: cost of two visas to Russia: 1,144 euro plus $90 online scam = $1,644.41 at the current conversion rate. It all seemed like a Seinfeld episode, particularly the part when I get doused with the muddy water.

We fly on Alitalia, in May, Florence to Rome and then Rome to St. Petersburg. Laura gave me her

Lonely Planet City Guide (our bible) as part of her "departure-from-Florence booty," and also her notes on St. Petersburg.

On our first night, we eat at The Idiot, the Dostoevsky-inspired cult favorite amongst St. Petersburg's artsy and ex-pat community, which Bill later pronounced his favorite restaurant of the trip, located at Naberezhnaya Reki Moyki, 82. It has a pre-Revolution atmosphere: four rooms decorated with antique furniture, oil paintings, and bookshelves, with fireplaces ablaze, and the availability of chess and backgammon sets. Bill orders an "Idiot Burger" and washes it down with a "Crime (ours) and Punishment (yours)," consisting of a vodka martini, cognac, and champagne. It arrives with a shot of vodka on the side, as does just about everything else. Whatever I ordered is too salty and the wine very expensive. I confess to not being all that partial to Russian cuisine; borscht, smelts, pickled herring, and vodka are not on my list of culinary favorites. We walk home along the Neva River after dinner at 10:45 p.m. in the twilight. It's getting close to "white nights," when it does not get dark at all.

We stay at the Grand Hotel Europe, which is beautiful, and indeed grand. We have a magnificent view of the Church on Spilled Blood from our window. The room comes with a buffet breakfast, which includes caviar, champagne, about 90 food stations and a harpist. The pitcher of dark liquid next to the pancakes looks like maple syrup, but Bill pours it over his breakfast only to find it is soy sauce. The Russians do love salt, which only adds to their unhealthy lifestyle of heavy smoking and even heavier drinking.

I am successful at getting the name and phone number of a St. Petersburg guide through a Florentine friend. We try the number and find she is available. Alla Yuskovets is a charming, funny woman of about 50 with a degree in Russian history. She is also walking encyclopedia of Russian art. Alla and a driver take us to Catherine's spectacular summer palace, followed by lunch in a church tower with only five tables. We pretend to not notice the obnoxious, loud American tourists at the other four tables.

She recommends a restaurant she thinks we will like. On our third night, we walk to the Petrograd side of the Neva River for a fabulous dinner of roasted duck with apples; it is a Russian and Soviet menu, complete with strolling gypsy musicians. It is very charming and the best food of the trip, with the exception of the lavish breakfast buffets.

We love the city, which reminds us of Venice with all the canals. The weather is mid-60s and sunny during the day, so we are very lucky. We log five miles (on my pedometer) in six hours at the Hermitage on our first visit. What a thrill it is to stand in rooms surrounded by paintings by Matisse (the famous *Dance*) and Cezanne! More important, when we return to the Hermitage with Alla, and subsequently to the Russian Museum, we learn so much about the great Russian painters of the 19th century, who had been largely overshadowed by their French counterparts of the time—names like Ilya Yefimovich Repin, Ivan Kramskoy and Vasily Perov.

Ralph Lauren (nee Lifshitz) is in St. Petersburg when we are there, on his way to Moscow to open his new (8,000-square-foot) flagship store and reclaim his Russian heritage. We do not see him, but we do have one celebrity citing at the Rome airport on our outbound flight; it is Willem Dafoe, who, like most movie stars, is shorter than he looks onscreen.

We have to go through two security checks at the airport when departing, the second one complete with "pat down." They want to know what the pedometer on my waist is. Only knowing two words in Russian, I have a hard time trying to explain that I have a goal of 10,000 steps a day—which I have far exceeded and loved every minute.

<hr />

After returning home to Florence from Russia, I start rewriting my novel that I began after my father died, *Time to Say Goodbye,* which the agent was unable to sell. In April I am drawn to an ad in *The Flo-*

rentine, the English-speaking news magazine: Tuscany Writers Conference—April 22-28. One of the top literary agents in America is going to be "agent in residence" in Lucca, just an hour-and-20-minute train ride from Florence. *What if I could meet her? What if I could give her my manuscript? What if she accepted it and sold it?* A couple of hours later I am already casting the movie version.

I email the conference to ask for the address. I have a hard copy of my recently completed and newly reworked manuscript with me, as well as a current resume. I will mail it. I wonder what kind of advance I will accept. Then I remember the first rule of sales: "Ninety percent of business is being there." I re-email the conference asking if I can come for a day. Tracey, who runs the conference, answers immediately and says I am welcome to come and can pay a fee for a day pass of 150 euros. She is even more accommodating when she offers to split the day. I can have dinner Sunday night, breakfast Monday, attend the opening talk, and stay for lunch.

I ask for hotels in the area around Lucca where the conference will be held. I receive yet another email from Tracey saying that one of the presenters at the conference would not be arriving until Tuesday, I was welcome to stay at an apartment at the villa for 65 euros a night, and yes, I was welcome to bring my husband. He could come to the dinner, of course, for no charge.

Bill and I arrive at the Florence train station in time to purchase the tickets for the 12:08 train to Lucca. By the time we reach the remote villa by taxi from the Lucca train station and check in to our countryside accommodations, we decide not to move. It is authentic Tuscany at its best. There is a kitchen, seating area, bedroom, and large bathroom. A huge gift basket awaits us, filled with local wine, olive oil, and biscotti from Lucca. Snacks are provided, plus water, wine, and cheese.

The rest of the group comes in little by little, with a few problems. Marty, from New York, had flown into Pisa and his luggage was lost. Tracey's lovely and helpful mother offers to wash Marty's clothes as he naps. She hangs them on the line to dry in the bright sun and then she irons them. He can't join us yet because he is naked in his room. Alan, book editor for AARP, is the first to join Bill and me as we sit at a table outside the villa enjoying a light snack and cold glass of white wine.

Tracey tells us that a group of Germans who were supposed to be coming were delayed in Frankfurt because the leader of the group had a heart attack. As the day goes on, they decide to cancel. By five o'clock, the agent's sister joins us; delightful, kooky, well-read, funny. Before I know it, as this small group sits around the table, a woman wearing a pink baseball hat, shorts, and a T-shirt plops in the chair next to me. "Hi, I'm Molly," she says. I have to contain

myself from falling all over her. I am hoping to un-
fold like a flower, petal by petal, and by the time she
realizes how funny and charming I am, she will beg
me for my manuscript.

Marty is among the last of the nine people who
join us Sunday night. He can't come until his clothes
are dry. Marty is 42 and one of the three managers
for Elton John, among others. He came to write because he was burned out from the whole New York
entertainment business. I name him "Marty-the-
one-man party."

Thus the crew includes the New York agent;
her sister from California; Alan, who is a presenter
along with Molly; Susan, writer, desperately seeking agent; Bill, supporting husband and companion; the now-clothed Marty, conference attendee;
and Sue, conference attendee who, when someone
calls her Sue an hour after she introduces herself
as such, says, "My name is Mindy; don't call me
Sue." Tracey and Donna are the conference helpers;
Donna is the amazingly kind and helpful mother of
Tracey.

We devour the Tuscan feast, consume bottles of
Chianti, and talk until very late. By the end of the
night we are tightly bonded, and I am feeling very
fortunate—and bold enough to implement my plan.
The next day I approach Molly after her class and
ask if she will read my manuscript. She says she
would be delighted to as she accepts the latest ver-

sion. Several hours pass, and sometime late in the afternoon she comes looking for me.

"There is such a disconnect between you and this manuscript," she said. "This could not have been written by the person I met yesterday. You're so much funnier and smarter in person! (*Was it the wine?*) You are many, many rewrites away from being anywhere with this." *She didn't like it; no, she hated it.*

We take the train back to Florence late that afternoon. Bill says the book is something I had to write for myself. "It is autobiographical and it was good you wrote it, but it is very personal. You don't write it to sell it. Besides," he continues, "I don't think she got it."

<hr />

Living in Florence makes travel so easy throughout Europe. It's so seductive when there's no ocean to cross. We planned to fly to London in August and meet up with Brian Johnson and two other friends. We would all take the train together to Brian's hometown of Newcastle, stay one night in a hotel, and drive to his good friend Brendan's wedding in Haydon Bridge, a charming village in Northumberland.

We were gathered in the lobby to leave for the wedding at 3 p.m. when Brian made his appearance in a traditional Scottish formal Highland dress kilt, complete with all accessories. Here was our friend without his skin-tight jeans, black T-shirt and signature herringbone-pattern flat cap, so I could not resist the photo opportunity. As I was focusing my camera, I backed up in my sling-back high heels, lost my balance, slid on the marble flooring and fell down the flight of stairs of the entranceway, arriving in a crumpled mass at the bottom. I hit my head and back and cut my right arm, but the worst is that I've twisted my ankle and my right foot and am in a lot of pain. With Bill's assistance, I hobble back to the room, take off the shoes, squeeze my feet into a pair of flat boots, get a bottle of Ibuprofen, a bag of ice, and we go on our way, six of us, all the time Brian and Bill saying we should go to the hospital. I do not want Brian to miss the wedding and I do not want to be responsible for all of us being late.

The magical ceremony takes place in a quaint, 12th-century church with 36 seats and no electricity. The bride stuns in a medieval-style high-waisted dress with a wreath of flowers in her hair, arriving in a horse drawn carriage, a sight truly out of a fairy tale. By the time we reach the reception, outside under a tent, and have some wine, I start to feel better. With Bill sensibly warning against it, I join in with a group doing an Irish step dance.

On the late night-return to the hotel my ankle throbs, and by the middle of the night, my now-elephantine foot and ankle are black and purple, the pain excruciating. Bill and I make it to Newcastle Hospital in the early morning, where we see a nurse practitioner who says she thinks I broke the bone in the far right part of my foot and sends me to X-ray. I picture myself hobbling around Florence in a cast with crutches. We are then told by another nurse who has inspected the films that it is not broken; it is soft tissue damage and it will take 6 weeks to heal. She gives me a compression stocking and tells me to take 1,200 mg of Ibuprofen daily along with 500mg Paracetamol (acetaminophen) caplets. There is no charge for any of this despite the fact that Bill keeps insisting on paying.

Back home, I am trying to maneuver potholes in the streets of Florence and taking 1,200 mg of Ibuprofen a day. My foot is still nasty-looking and somewhat swollen. The day we were leaving England, the Newcastle paper had a story about medical mishaps at the hospital, including photos of people who died from a doctor removing the healthy kidney instead of the damaged one, incorrect medication and other disasters. I feel lucky to have escaped further harm.

La Donna da Sardinia

We have a cleaning lady from Sardinia, Piera, who calls me Kelley. I don't mind that she calls me by my last name. For the last few years on her weekly cleaning visits she has invited us to her house for Sunday dinner. We finally decide that we have to accept. We take a taxi to the outskirts of the city and arrive at a group of gray, nondescript concrete buildings. We meet Piera's husband and son, who, although engaged for 18 years, lives at home with his parents most of the time.

Piera has roasted a pig and has brought vacuum-packed cheese from Sardinia to Florence. The feast goes on for hours. Piera, her husband and son do not speak any English, so we converse in our best Italian and it works out that our communication skills are okay. We learn that the boys are quite spoiled by their mothers in most of Italy, and see no need to leave home. The young Italian women are looking for careers and not anxious for marriage or anyone to take care of—especially a husband.

I quit the gym. Last year, I went five days a week, did the treadmill half an hour, lifted weights and used all the fancy machines. End result? Nothing buttoned and my thighs looked as big as Arnold Schwarzenegger's. I found a Pilates studio that is part of a rehab facility. Not only is it high-tech, with all the latest equipment, but it's a 20-minute walk at a fast pace and that means many steps on my pedometer—around 5,000 round trip. So I get the Pilates, a brisk walk and since no one speaks English, I get the bonus Italian lesson.

I have no intention of rejoining the International League of Florence, a non-profit organization (dedicated to fund raising for charity), but they are offering small-group Italian lessons through the Dante Alighieri School twice a week for two hours at a very reasonable rate. The class consists of four women roughly the same age and level as me. It's perfect; none of us can remember anything. One woman is from Toronto, very nice and smart, and another is an Australian whose husband is the priest at the American church, St. Stephen's.

One day in conversation class she was trying to come up with the vocabulary for her *merito* (husband), Roger, being stabbed (*pugnalare*). He's okay, but a homeless guy asked him for money when he was taking out the trash. The church gives food and clothing to the vagrants, but no money, as they generally use it for drugs. Roger was not badly injured, but the blunt instrument punctured his skin by his shoulder. Next day he was in shock and experienced chills and vomited (*vomitato*).

The fourth and final member of the class is an American woman who reeks of perfume, is dressed head to toe in Versace, and arrives in full makeup at 9 a.m. This has the effect of making the rest of us all look rather frumpy. Nevertheless, we are in it together, hoping for the same outcome; a better ability to speak the beautiful Italian language.

We decide to take further advantage of our proximity to wonderful European cities, and book a trip to Berlin. Our young ballerina friend, Anina, will be there, and has offered to give us a tour. At the suggestion of a good friend, I decide to treat us to a stay at the Hotel Adlon Kempinski, in the heart of the city, next to the most famous landmark in Berlin, the Brandenburg Gate.

The weather is brutally cold for November. Anina proves a good friend and a tireless guide and she takes us to the many sections of the city, on and off buses and trains. We spend a day at Museum Island, the location of five world-renowned museums gathered in an extraordinary ensemble, including the Pergamonmuseum, Haus am Checkpoint Charlie, and the very moving Memorial to the Murdered Jews of Europe.

Berlin has some of the finest museums in the world. Many collections previously split between East and West Berlin have been brought together in new venues. We find it to be a sprawling and bustling city, filled with young people.

After returning to Florence, we find out that our cleaning lady Piera has to have a knee replacement, so she is now bringing along her son's *fianciata,* of 18 years, to help her clean. I prefer just Piera but under the circumstances, I have no choice. The most apparent problem is that she has a different way of cleaning; she puts everything in drawers and closets and we can't find anything *and* she has switched cleaning products.

We are invited to a "going away party" for our friends Gina and Ed, who are leaving after three years, on a Friday when Piera has just finished cleaning. I arrive home at 5:30 to shower and change. I am washing my hair when a speck of something seems to jump from the showerhead into my eye, which I thought was closed. I think it must be an eyelash but it begins to burn. I get out of the shower and run water from the sink over my eye, but it is getting worse. I call Bill at his studio and ask him to come home and help me. He arrives right away and pours bottles of water over my eyes, but I am still in agony.

We call Dr. Dave, my daughter's husband in the States who is an ER doctor. He says we were doing the right thing, but still there is no relief. We do not go to the party, as I cannot open my eye. I finally take Advil PM and go to sleep, because I am in too much pain to go to the hospital emergency room. The next day I go to an English-speaking ophthalmologist on the outskirts of the city center. He appears concerned, but after careful examination tells me I have an abrasion on the cornea, most probably caused by rubbing my eye when whatever thing flew in it from the recently cleaned showerhead. He gives me a prescription for eye drops and his cell number, in case I have further problems. The pain has subsided but now my eye is itching. I probably am particularly scared because we have just heard that Bill's 92-year-old aunt had to have her eye removed at Massachusetts Eye and Ear due to an infection. But once again I have escaped a serious injury in Italy.

The spring of 2008 is bitter sweet. Our lease will be ending June 30, on both our apartment on Borgo degli Albizi and the studio on the Ponte Vecchio. A combination of things precipitated our need to return to the States to regroup. We have a lot going on in the art business. What started with a commitment of "one semester" has turned into nine years of living here and full immersion into Florentine culture.

Bill's conversion to full-time artist is so successful that he has been contacted by a Denver-based art advisor, who wants to do a PBS video of him at his studio in Sarasota in the fall. He is also scheduled for his fourth solo art exhibition at the Wickiser Gallery in New York City. Our dreams have been fulfilled from the art point of view.

We have to take a sabbatical from Florence for a year but we know we will be back. However, I do not know at the time that the seed of our return will start when I take Bill to Paris for his 65th birthday.

We enjoy our remaining time in Florence now more than ever. Brian Johnson and his wife Brenda come in May to visit. Brian has just finished a successful album with AC/DC in Vancouver and wants to see his buddy. He says he wants to take my husband shopping: "Come on, Billy, we'll do *Queer Eye for the Straight Guy*." They walk down Borgo degli Albizi arm in arm; Brian is unrecognizable without his trademark cap. His wife Brenda and I catch up with them at Avirex on Via del Corso, a corner store describing itself as, "Civilian & Military Tailors." Next to the sign is a framed black-and-white photo of Steve McQueen wearing a brown leather aviator bomber jacket.

The boys are having a hilarious time and Brian is entertaining the young proprietor of the shop. Bill stands to the side, dressed in a brown plaid madras jacket and cargo pants next to a pile of shirts and pants that are accumulating by the cash register, none of which look like anything he would ever wear. Brenda exclaims, "Billy, you look so hot!" My husband turns to the eager salesman: "*Prendo tutti!*" ("I'll take everything!")

———⊗⊗⊗———

A few days after our friends return to London, we meet Lisa at the Ristorane and Wine Bar dei Frescobaldi on via dei Magazzini for lunch. She walks in, huffing and puffing as she lowers herself into the armchair. "I hate my husband," she exhales. "Really?" Bill says. "What a surprise." We've heard this for 10 years and if we dare to agree with Lisa, she jumps to the defense of Marcello. She laughs at Bill's sarcasm. Her social life is not what it used to be in Florence. She is heading to New York for more treatments for her eye problems; she's spending more time in the States now.

When our Florentine odyssey began nine years ago, Bill knew his fellow students and his art teachers. We met just about everyone else we know in Florence because of Lisa. She is the single source of every social thing we have done in Florence and Positano for all these years. She introduced us to Suzanne, our realtor and good friend, and to the Frescobaldi family and of course Keith at the Florence Dance Center. We even spent an evening with Robocop at her villa in Positano.

The Art of Provence

Living in Florence, we are surrounded by arguably the greatest paintings and sculptures in
the world—Michelangelo's *David* at the Galleria
dell'Accademia, and of course, the Uffizi, the oldest gallery in the world. There is a fresco in the entranceway of our palazzo condo that tourists try to
photograph through the gate on a daily basis, and
we have restored frescoes in our bedroom. But my
husband's appetite for art and its history is insatia-
ble, and that is why we decide to drive to the south
of France and check out the spots where some of the
great modern masters have lived and painted.

By Googling MapQuest, I find the drive to Nice,
on the Cote d'Azur, will only take 4 1/2 hours. That
is, if you don't have to get out of the Hertz garage
and beyond the city of Florence, which is a maze of
construction and one-way streets.

A couple of hours safely out of the city on a warm
May Saturday, I struggle to figure out the air con-
ditioning system in our rented four-door Fiat Punto.
With great effort, I read the manual using my limited
Italian technology vocabulary. I think, *Why didn't we
pay the extra 5 euros for a bigger car?* But I decide not

to mention it to my husband, who is maneuvering the gearshift. I feel like I am riding a bucking bronco.

"Isn't this great?" he says as my neck snaps back and then forward. "I love a manual shift." His enthusiasm for just about everything life has to offer is not always reciprocated. We stop at a gas station on the Autostrada and explain our dilemma. The serviceman sticks his head in the car, studies the instruction book, puts up the hood, and continues his inspection. He invites the other station attendants to join him. Then, frowning with intent concern, he says that we do not have air conditioning. *"Si,"* they all chime in. We drive the rest of the way, through numerous tunnels, with the windows open, hair blowing in our eyes and mouths, reassuring ourselves it's okay because we'll find a Hertz office in France and change cars.

We arrive in Nice, where it takes another 45 minutes to locate the Hotel Windsor at 11 Rue Dalpozzo, a recommendation of friends who have lived in this city for a decade. They steered us away from the massive Hotel Negresco and to this "boutique hotel," which markets itself as a *"Rendezvous avec l'art."* "Sleep in the company of your favorite artist." I already do. There is original artwork in our bedroom and a lovely balcony overlooking the garden.

Nice is France's largest tourist resort and fifth biggest city. The Windsor is an ideal location, just a couple of blocks from the Promenade des Anglais, the main boulevard along the water with numerous brasseries and restaurants. We notice many French people drinking rosé—something you would not see in Florence.

Sunday morning, after breakfast in the hotel garden, we set out on a very long walk to the Musee Matisse, once home to the great painter. It is located in a 17th-century Genoese villa painted a pomegranate red with golden yellow trim, set in the middle of a beautiful park. The museum displays works of Matisse and some of his contemporaries. We find it delightfully intimate.

On the walk back we find a Hertz office. We explain our problem and they very nicely tell us that they cannot change our car because it is from another country. We continue to the sea and have a well-deserved lunch at Ruhl Plage, a beach restaurant with a charmingly friendly waiter who asks where we are from. When my husband says he is originally from Boston, the tanned, youthful waiter says, "Red Sox, Celtics, Patriots!" He used to have a girlfriend from New Haven, Connecticut, he explains.

After two days we leave Nice, MapQuest directions in hand, and drive the short distance to our second stop, the beautiful medieval hilltop village of Saint-Paul-de-Vence. Our destination here is the Hotel Colombe d'Or. When I read that many famous literati and glitterati flocked to Saint-Paul, then saw the photo of Simone Signoret and Yves Montand seated in the courtyard in front of the hotel and read that they'd had their wedding reception here, I knew I had to go. I sold Bill on the fact that the hotel houses one of the finest 20th-century private art collections, built up over time in lieu of payment of bills by such famous artists as Miro, Picasso, Chagall, and Braque.

It is even more charming and beautiful than we expected. The unobtrusive entrance takes us through the garden, where lunch is being served. A man appears, takes our bags out of the car, and drives off to the car park.

We walk around the narrow meandering streets, which are filled with shops and numerous art galleries. This is about as opposite from Nice as one could imagine. We sit at Café de la Place and watch elderly gentlemen playing a game of petanque or boules, a first cousin of the Italian bocce. The aim is to roll a number of hollow steel balls as close as possible to a small wooden target ball.

The views are stunning, and Bill starts to sketch immediately. At dinner that evening, in the world-renowned restaurant of the hotel, we admire a breathtaking array of original paintings. We dine at a corner table beneath a Picasso. Our room also has original sketches, as well as a terrace that overlooks colorful roof tiles of vibrant yellow, blue, and red to the large swimming pool, where a Calder sculpture dominates. As I close my eyes for the night, I wonder if Simone and Yves slept in this same bed.

Next stop is Aix-en-Provence. Aix is a cosmopolitan student hub with grand boulevards and one of the oldest universities in Europe, dating back to 1409. This is Cezanne country, and we stay at the newly refurbished Hotel Cezanne. Since Sister Wendy has called my husband "the spiritual son to Cezanne," Cezanne's hometown is the ultimate place for us to visit. After lunch we make an appointment with the tourist office for a private showing at his studio—a cottage in a garden.

Cezanne's last studio, which he designed himself, is preserved as it was at the time of his death in 1906, complete with personal belongings and his furniture. It is strewn with his brushes, easel, tools and still-life arrangements, along with some sketches and drawings. He worked here every day for the last four years of his life. It is an overwhelming experience to stand where he painted many famous works, including his last, *Large Bathers*. I can feel his presence intensely, as can my husband, who is quiet and reverent. As we leave, we buy a ceramic copy of the olive pot Cezanne used in several of his works. We stroll through the Old Town in silence, back to the Cours Mirabeau, the main boulevard, and to one of Cezanne's favorite places, Cafe des Deux Garcons, where he would meet his friends for drinks at the end of the day.

The next day we drive a short distance outside of the city to Le Tholonet and to the base of La Montagne Ste-Victoire, the mountain Cezanne painted over and over again. We climb a hill and Bill finds the perfect flat rock where he can lay his sketchpad and mix paint colors—shades of the clay at the base of the mountain, the deeper tint of the quarries, the colors of the mountain itself. I collect a handful of the terracotta earth and roll it in paper so he will have the exact color when he returns to his studio in Florence. Many people talk about the light in Provence, and it does seem especially radiant.

We have a quiet, spectacular dinner at Amphityron on Rue Doumer in the outside garden. The "spiritual son to Cezanne" is content. He has inspiration and mental images to take home to paint.

We leave Aix reluctantly after two days and make the one-hour drive to the town of Arles. This is Van Gogh country. The hotel of choice is the historic Grand Hotel Nord-Pinus, overlooking the central square, where Van Gogh painted the *Cafe de Nuit*. This hotel is a national monument, and many painters have stayed here. We go straight to the Café for lunch. Bill sits and sketches. I talk about the light. Everything seems to look better. I certainly do. It's a soft, flat, even light that creates no harsh shadows, and has the same effect as a pink light bulb.

We pick up a map at the tourist office and a brochure in English and set out along "the Van Gogh trail"—a walking circuit of the city marked by a foot-path embedded with plaques marking spots where Van Gogh placed his easel to paint canvases such as *Starry Night Over the Rhone* (1880). At each stop, there is a photo of the painting, along with pertinent information. We walk along the banks of the Rhone River, following the footsteps. Van Gogh's *Little Yellow House,* which he painted in 1888, was destroyed during WWII, but a life-size replica of his bedroom, which he sketched and painted several times, is set up as a small museum, *La Chambre de Vincent.* For a nominal admission, we are able to climb the stairs for the view. I take photos, and they are practically indistinguishable from the original Van Gogh painting; side by side, it would be a tough call.

On our second day in Arles we take a day trip to explore some of the nearby small towns. Our first stop is our farthest point in Provence, Chateauneuf du Pape, an adorable town with many wine shops. We stop to breathe in the crisp, clean mountain air. We have some tea and visit a few vineyards. We find out that 2005 was the best year in over 20 years for the wine. Naturally, we pick up a few bottles. There are many vistas to paint. "I have another 10 years of canvases in my head, just from this trip," my husband says. "I can't wait to get back and start painting."

Roman ruins surround the countryside of Aix-en-Provence and Arles. We drive through the medieval city of Avignon, which was the center of the Roman Catholic world from 1309 until 1377, when the papacy temporarily abandoned Italy. Seven French popes reigned. The miniature Vatican, Palais des Papes, a grand fortress-like palace bordered by the Rhone, testifies to the fact that they led a very grand life.

Our next stop is Saint-Remy-de-Provence, a beautiful and charming town, with shops that sell lavender everything: fresh lavender, dried lavender, lavender soap and perfume, as well as pottery, Provençal fabrics, and amazing handmade chocolates.

We stop at Joel Durand Chocolatier, and buy chocolate bars, 70 percent cacao, and a tremendous assortment of dark, filled candies, each marked with a letter describing what is inside. Later we have the dark chocolates with a sip of Chateuneuf du Pape— an unbeatable combination. Saint-Remy was home to Nostradamus, the 16th-century physician and astrologer, who was born in a house still standing on Avenue Hoche in the old quarter. Too bad he missed out on the chocolates by a few centuries.

Next, on the road to Les Baux, we stop at Clinique St-Paul, the mental hospital where Van Gogh went after he mutilated his ear. The hospital stands as it does in his paintings, sprawling and tinted a soft yellow. Several months after he left the asylum, in 1890, he shot himself, at the age of 37. Bill and I find it eerie to linger in the field where he painted many of his final landscapes.

In fact, Bill is so agitated that when he backs up the car, he first hits a rock and then a tree as he tries to keep the Fiat from tumbling into a ditch. We now have a rear depression and a dent on the right fender and a broken hubcap. For the rest of the trip, I refer to him as "Crash Kelley."

Our last stop before returning to Arles is Les Baux-de-Provence, a dramatic fortress site renowned for its white bauxite cliffs. Emmanuel, the manager of the Grand Nord-Pinus, has told us that we must go to the *cathedrale* and see the Van Gogh show, a short drive from the town. Produced by Regis Prevot, *Cathedrale d'Images* is a series of images projected on the naturally white walls and even the stony floor of a massive bauxite cave.

We watch the slide show of Van Gogh and his works with musical accompaniment by Bach, entranced by this labor of love. We return to Arles for our final night and drink rosé wine along with the others at the *Café de Nuit*.

On the drive back to Florence (eight hours from Arles), we pass Cannes. The film festival is in full swing, and even though we are anxious for a peek at Brad and Angelina, there are no available rooms. Cannes is known as a place to avoid during the festival, as it is overrun with an additional 30,000 people: stars with their entourages, directors, producers, journalists, and other "hangers on." Nevertheless, we are sorry to miss a chance to gaze at Hollywood stars.

We are tired and it is a long ride back to Florence. We drive about 150 miles, much of it through tunnels, it seems, and finally approach the last exit before Florence, where we stop to fill up the diesel tank and assess the damages to the car.

Bill gets down on his hands and knees and eases himself under the car. Holding the bumper in his right hand, and using language as colorful as his paintings, he manages to punch out all the dents with his left fist. "It's all plastic," he says in amazement. He sees the blood trickling down his arm and carefully inspects the cuts. Now he's not so sure he did the right thing. "Well, at least it's not my painting hand," he says. "And we won't have to buy the car." We treat the wounds with Purel hand sanitizer. "I'll bet Cezanne didn't have these problems," he says, as we pay the final toll.

Intermission

It is time to remove our belongings from our home of four years and return to Florida. We will sorely miss our Italian friends. I walk around the city and reflect on our years here and the people we know, and I look at everything as if for the first time—or the last.

I will miss my ancient little church, *Chiesa di Santa Margherita de' Cerchi*, also known as the Church of Dante on via Santa Margherita, across the street from the Casa di Dante Museum dedicated to the poet and to *The Divine Comedy*. Tradition says that Dante met his muse Beatrice here for the first time and fell in love with her. The intimate, peaceful church, with just a few wooden benches, dates back to 1032 and houses what tradition identifies as the tomb of Dante's great love, Beatrice Portinari. In front of the tomb is a basket full of messages that lovers write to Beatrice, asking her to protect their love; the basket is always overflowing.

We invite our realtor friend, Suzanne, to dinner and deliver our news of leaving Florence and the apartment. We are certain she'll be devastated to see us go. Without missing a beat, she says "Can I show it tomorrow?"

⸺∞⸺

I always go over-the-top for Bill's birthday. His daughter says he's the only person over the age of five who requires an annual party. In 2009 he will be 65, and I want something unique—unlike the usual merrymaking with friends (the 50th) or a celebration with adult children and the ever-growing brood of grandkids (the 60th). My epiphany comes when I see online that AC/DC is scheduled to play in Paris. Now I only have to figure out how to put the trip together *and* keep it a surprise.

I start by checking the band schedule online to see if Brian Johnson will be available for Bill's birthday. For 18 years, I've always checked with him first before setting the party date, and have put him in charge of Bill's timely arrival when it's a surprise. More often than not, Brian has blown it: "See you at your surprise party tomorrow, mate."

When I see that the band is playing in Paris on Bill's birthday, February 25, it is, as my husband would call it, "a no brainer."

I block out the time on Bill's calendar and tell him to make no plans. "Just be home by noon on the 19th." He asks, "How will I know what to pack, if I don't know where I'm going?" I tell him I will pack for him, and that is all he needs to know. For the next few months, he frequently asks, "So, where am I going?" My response is to hum from the Beach Boys song *Kokomo*: "*Aruba, Jamaica, oooh, I wanna take ya . . .*"

Brian has a brief break around Christmas and is back in Sarasota. One night when Bill is out of hearing distance, he tells me, "It's fucking fabulous, me darlin'. We'll take Billy with the band by motorcade to the concert! You can come, too," he adds—jokingly, I hope.

As the weeks pass, it is increasingly difficult to keep the secret. One evening, as we are getting ready to go out for dinner, Bill suggests we take a short trip to visit his aunt, a four-hour drive away. "I can't take any trips before France," I say. *Oh my God, did he hear me? Did I blow my own surprise? Wait, don't panic. What rhymes with France . . . chance. Okay, I can do this.*

I walk to the bedroom and say, "Sorry, but I just don't think I can *chance* a short trip before the big one; I have too much to do." He shrugs and says, "Okay, maybe March." *That was close.*

I order *Eyewitness Travel*, *Top 10 Paris*, and *Rick Steves's Paris 2009* from Amazon and I buy a beret. I keep them all well-hidden.

The day arrives and so does Bill—returning home from his studio at the designated time. I have a taxi pick us up and take us to Sarasota airport. Once we arrive I tell him to go inside, and I explain the situation to the porter. He becomes part of the plan as he checks the three bags to Paris and looks at our passports as Bill stands inside the automatic door, hands in pockets. Once seated onboard, my artist says, "When do I find out where you're taking me?" "When we get to Atlanta," I tell him.

So we deplane in Atlanta, I check the flight, and we are off to Gate 36 for an on-time departure. We walk by the gate marked "Florence," and my husband looks kind of nostalgic—or is he disappointed we are not going to Italy? Next we pass Panama City, and he breathes a sigh of relief. Mexico City comes up and his body visibly stiffens; it's not his favorite place, but he knows one of my brothers lives there. Then he spots the lighted sign before I do.

"Paris?" He smiles. "I love Paris!"

I don my beret and give him his first two gifts, the Paris guidebooks. As the plane speeds down the runway, he tells me how surprised he is and asks, "Why Paris?" I tell him he will find out in due time.

We arrive at The Hôtel Lutetia, on the Boulevard Raspail, in Saint-Germain-des-Prés. We have been upgraded to a charming suite with a balcony off the bedroom and another off the sitting room. I am feeling relieved that so far the trip has gone as planned. Later, we decide to have a drink in the cozy bar. Bill settles into his comfortable leather armchair and orders a brandy. "Why are we here?"

I am amazed and delighted that he doesn't seem suspicious. I tell him to wait as I go to our room for the next clues. I return moments later and hand him a package, which he quickly opens. It contains a photo of Brian performing onstage, earplugs, the AC/DC *Black Ice* CD from their current tour, and AC/DC undershorts (the last two items I had to go to Walmart to purchase).

"What are these for?" he asks. *He must be tired.* "Is Brian in Paris?"

I explain the situation of "Why Paris?" Today is Friday, and the concert is next Wednesday—his birthday. So I tell him I have made reservations for lunch at the Jules Verne restaurant at the Eiffel Tower on his birthday, and at night we will go to the AC/DC concert with the band—via police escort. Clearly, he is stunned. I can now relax as we wrap up our arrival day in Paris with dinner at the Brasserie Lutetia.

We spend the following days at the Louvre and Musée d'Orsay and other favorite places. Day 4, Monday, we have reserved for a trip to Montmartre and the Sacre Coeur Basilica. We take a taxi, as there is a fine mist in the air and it is damp and cool. The driver drops us at the foot of the church, and we walk up Rue de Steinkerque past souvenir shops ("I Love Paris" T-shirts and ashtrays) before arriving at the white marble church. We sit at a café trying to warm up with an Irish coffee and watch an artist complete a small, colorful canvas of the famed Moulin Rouge.

Bill decides we should buy it and refuses to negotiate the price. "Never offend an artist by offering less than he asks." The artist happily pockets the euros, wraps up the painting for us, breaks down his easel, and heads to a nearby bar. He is done for the day.

We arrive back at our hotel after a brief stop at Harry's Bar, promising ourselves a quick nap. But we find two messages from Brian, who has just arrived in town from his show in Sweden. He wants us to meet him in half an hour at the Four Seasons Hotel bar. We do a quick turnaround and are out the door and into a cab. Sure enough, fans are positioned in groups outside the hotel, awaiting any glimpse of a band member.

We meet in the bar, and after getting caught up over an exquisite bottle of Montrachet, we head out into a beautiful Paris evening with Brian; his wife, Brenda, who has just arrived from the states; Cliff, the bass guitarist; and Brian's tour trainer, Nick. As Brian artfully dodges fans seeking autographs, the band's tour manager guides us to Chez André, an upscale neighborhood bistro.

We pass under the red awning that stretches over an array of shellfish on ice and into this atmospheric French landmark. Cliff and Brian order frogs' legs as a starter. And we all have steak-frites, which are authentic and delicious. Bill couldn't be happier.

The next day, Wednesday, February 25, the long-anticipated and overly planned birthday has arrived.

We have a lazy morning and take a taxi to the Eiffel Tower. We go to the south pillar of the Tower, under the yellow awning, as directed, and they check our name. We take the private elevator to Le Jules Verne. The restaurant is considered one of the best in Paris, and is under the direction of the great chef restaurateur Alain Ducasse. The atmosphere is romantic, and we are ushered to a window table, as I had requested. The food and wine are exceptional and the vista—the entire city of Paris!—is stupendous. By the time we walk back to the hotel, it is almost time to meet Brian and the band at the Four Seasons.

Two giant drivers, Peter and Gunther, await us, as do two equally colossal tour managers, Tim and Daryl. This has an overall comical effect, as Angus and Malcolm, the other band members, are barely five feet tall and weigh about ninety pounds each. As we stand in the lobby, I say to Brian, "They're so tiny."

"We're small people," he says. "I look like fucking Tarzan next to them."

The tour manager explains that the hotel entrance is packed with fans. He tells us that when he calls our names, we must run out the door and directly into the vans.

"Brian, Brenda, go!" he yells, and they take off speedily. "Susan, Bill, go!" he hollers, and we follow.

Paparazzi are snapping photos, and crowds of people of all ages are begging for autographs. As instructed, we look straight ahead as we duck into the vehicle. We feel like we are traveling with the Beatles as we speed off, fans banging on the windows and flashes going off, and we are on our way to the Palais Omnisports de Paris-Bercy.

We are in the third van, led by two police officers on motorcycles, their bubble lights flashing as we speed down the right lane past the thick traffic—rocking and rolling down the Champs-Elysées. Bill beams, his face flushed with delight. Visibility at last!

Half an hour later, we enter an underground garage. The tour manager opens our door and leads us to the reception room, where several invited people are waiting—mostly band relatives and friends, and a few journalists. He gives us our black-and-red *Black Ice* World Tour guest passes to be worn on a cord around our neck.

We hang around for a while before we are led to our stage-left seats. The venue, which holds 17,000, is sold out, and the audience is whooping and clapping loudly and waving red lights. Some are wearing sponge horns to simulate the lead guitar player, Angus, when the band sings "Hell's Bells." Next to Bill is a super fan. He's tall, well over six feet, and dressed like Angus, in a velvet Eton suit with short pants. He's as excited as a toddler on sugar overload, jumping up and down, arms and hands flailing about. I'm hoping he doesn't drop his pants—Angus does as part of the act.

The band comes on stage at around 9 p.m., and the audience erupts in a frenzy. The front floor, by the stage, is standing room, so about every 10 minutes the crowd passes a body over the top of the masses to the police, who gently lead the person to what looks like a holding pen. If the fan is really out of control, he or she is seated in a wheelchair and talked to, but it is all very civil.

Part of the set is a huge train with steam coming out, featured in the song "Rock 'N' Roll Train." A fat, mostly naked blow-up doll inflates slowly from the ceiling as the band chants, "A Whole Lotta Rosie." The sound is relentless, the production awesome, and Brian sounds really good. I am amazed at how many people know all the lyrics (sparse as they are) to every song. The superfan goes totally nuts singing "Big Jack"—I think those are the *only* lyrics.

For over two hours the music reverberates as the band thumps out the songs, all the while running the full length of the stage and down the center runway into the audience, and leading it all, is our friend Brian. He spots Bill from the side of the stage and gives him a smile and a nod. The drummer, Phil, cigarette dangling from his lips, is the only seated band member. For the grand finale, gigantic real cannons are rolled out and shoot several rounds of deafening booms. The band blasts, "For Those of You About to Rock, We Salute You."

The energy expended by the band is exhilarating—it's impossible not to get swept up in the general mania—and whether you like the music or not, who couldn't love "You Shook Me All Night Long"? We dance and shake like teenagers. But *ow*, my feet, my hips, my back! We're not teenagers, alas, and I know we'll be feeling the effects in the morning. *How does Brian do it?* I wonder for the umpteenth time.

Afterward we meet back in the reception room, where each band member is presented with a double platinum album from Sony Records in France. TV cameras are everywhere. Phil, the somber, chain-smoking drummer, approaches. "Hi, Bill—I just wanted to wish you a happy birthday," he says. Angus mumbles something unintelligible. "How did you like the royal box?" Brian asks, referring to our seats.

Brian's brother Maurice, a fabulous chef, has cooked for the band, but Brian takes his food to go. The drivers herd us into the vehicles and back to the hotel.

"I'm having too much fun," Bill says. "Is my birthday over yet?"

We pull up in front of the Four Seasons; hundreds of hopeful fans being held back by hotel security lunge at the van. Brian is holding onto the food his brother gave him. I tell Brian that he is the star and can't really get out of the car carrying a Tupperware-covered dish of food. "Right," he says, handing it to Bill. "You carry it."

Brian invites us back to his suite, and we happily accept. We are having a drink as the sweet aroma of marijuana fills the air, and someone passes me a joint. Although I have not smoked one since college, I get teased into taking a hit as it goes around. We are not even smokers—but hey, it's Paris, and it is a special occasion. Suddenly my back no longer hurts! I can see why they prescribe this stuff to people with chronic pain. We then proceed to clean out the mini bar—eating and drinking everything.

At last we get back into the van and head for our hotel. As we say goodbye, Brian turns and lowers his voice. "Hey," he says, "We'll always have Paris."

The tour driver delivers us back to our Left Bank hotel. It is 3 a.m. You're never too old to party with rock stars.

With the birthday and the thrill of the concert behind us, we are free to continue with our art tour. Bill has his heart set on exploring Musée de l'Orangerie in the Jardin des Tuileries. He wants to see Claude Monet's masterworks, the *Nymphéas* (Water Lilies), painted in the artist's garden at Giverny. Monet stipulated that the monumental panels be displayed precisely as they are seen today, in and oval room with massive paintings facing each other that surround viewers with his vision of beauty.

We sit on the long oval bench, which mirrors the shape of the room, and are captivated by the sheer size of the works; 2x5 meter panels. "I think I can do with landscapes what Monet did with water lilies," Bill says. But the only place I can paint a massive painting like this is Florence." And just like that, it is decided that we will return to our favorite city.

Having gone to Paris for the Maestro's 65th birthday, we realize that despite all that Paris has to offer, we are longing for Italy. There will be a 90th birthday for my mother in the spring that took a year of planning. And Bill has another show in New York, so we make plans to return to Florence in the fall. We will need to find a place to live and for Bill to paint. We can't stay away any longer.

Our Renaissance

Until the week before we leave for Florence in September 2009, I had hoped we would be able to rent our old place on Borgo degli Albizi, but at the last minute, they had a long-term booking. "Don't worry, there's always a better deal," Bill says. And he turns out to be right.

By luck, a magnificent apartment on Via Oriuolo becomes available. I had requested an apartment with two bedrooms and two bathrooms, with a terrace. I looked at the stunning pictures online and booked it for a month, not knowing if we would like it.

We arrive to find something even more spectacular than the photos indicated. It is a large, attractively furnished apartment on the top floor with breathtaking views of the Duomo from every window. This apartment has an interior elevator that leads to a top floor, the *piccionaia* (pigeon's roost), a large furnished room with a skylight and a door that leads to a massive roof deck with a 360-degree panoramic view of Florence. You can almost reach out and touch the Duomo; it is a perfect studio for the Maestro. The main floor has two long terraces, a living room, dining room, a master bedroom and en suite bathroom, and a guest bedroom and bath.

A bonus for me is that Bill can now be home for lunch. This will be our home every fall for as long as we want, the manager tells us. There is a large lower-level game room with laundry, but of, course, no dryer. It is large enough for Bill to use to paint his massive landscape. "I'm never leaving," he says. "See if we can extend."

I have negotiated a deal that includes a week- ly cleaning woman who also brings freshly pressed Frette bed linens. You can imagine that with no clothes dryer, washing and drying sheets is a com- plex inconvenience. I used to have to take them out and have them professionally washed and ironed.

Bill returns to the glass store on Via del Procon- solo. Here, at Migliorini Giuseppe e Figlio, he orders two large pieces of glass that will become this year's palettes. After several trips to buy supplies at Zec- chi, Florence's number one art store, just south of the Duomo on a street called Via del Studio—so named because for centuries it has also been the home of some major art studios—my husband is ready to work. During our years here, we have gotten to know all the wonderful people that work at Zecchi, includ- ing Massimo, the owner, a very nice man, who comes to visit and see Bill's work at the end of each season.

Bill starts to paint downstairs. He challenges himself and starts the first giant, 7x15-foot Italian landscape of Panzano Valley (the size of Monet's *Water Lilies* in Musée de l'Orangerie, Paris, which are 3 panels of this same size). Bill's idea is to start with one. When Massimo Zecchi, sees the painting, he becomes very emotional and names it *Anima della Toscana*—Tuscan Soul.

After finishing this very large landscape, Bill starts another painting not quite so large (5x7- foot); a totally different vista—a Tuscan scene of olive trees that is in the vicinity of Poggio Antico, a winery that we had visited outside of Montalcino. This painting is not so much a vista, it is more like standing in the midst of the vineyard—a totally different composition. You can almost touch the olive trees. After completing this, he sends a photo to Sister Wendy. She comments, "What a triumph. This work is alive with color and space. One is drawn in and held in peaceful joy."

Now finished with being a successful relationship guru, and having sustained a failed attempt as a novelist, I am writing a book of humorous essays about the challenges of middle age, our attempts at maintenance and staying visible, my appearance on *The Oprah Winfrey Show*, adult children, aging parents and traveling with 13 pairs of black pants. I title it, *I Oprahed*. I have an agent in New York who has agreed to read it.

We work contentedly and at the end the day, relax with a first glass of wine, listen to Andrea Bocelli, and go out to our favorite neighborhood *trattoria*. We are happily at home in Florence, and although we were gone a year, it is as though we never left. Not much changes in the city. When we returned to Café Rivoire for our first *aperitivo,* our old friend and favorite waiter greeted us; *"Buon estate?"* Salvatore asks. Good summer?

My saddest experience in Florence took place only days after we moved into the new apartment. I noticed the apartment was missing a few essentials, which I decided to pick up at the local hardware store. As I left our building in the morning and took a left turn on Via dell' Oriuolo, I was carrying a bag of garbage to deposit in the nearest dumpster. Florence has a do-it-yourself garbage system here, which means there are no pick-ups and we have to find a dumpster as close to where we live as possible. I heard a loud thud, and saw a man lying on the street. Everything happened so fast, I assumed the person had been hit by a car. The victim appeared to be dressed in colorful clothes with something wrapped about his or her head. My immediate thought is that it is one of the gypsy beggars. Then I noticed a man pointing up to a window and excitedly relating what happened to a passerby.

A few shopkeepers come out side to see what the commotion is about. The street is lined with artisan shops, carpenters, jewelers, and frame-makers, and is two blocks from the Duomo, which looms at the end of the street. Spectators stare at the body on the street and then look up to the window. Hands are gesturing everywhere amidst animated chatter. I move a little closer, garbage in hand. A man calls the police from his cell phone. Soon sirens scream down the narrow street, and policemen on motor-cycles arrive within minutes. The victim is, appar-ently, *morto*. The body is prodded and poked by sev-eral officious-looking people—but it lies like a limp rag doll, lifelessly in the street. I cross to the other side of the street. I don't have the heart to open the dumpster and toss the bag, so I just keep walking. The crowd continues to build.

Two hours later, I return and the body is still in the street, which has now become an official crime scene, complete with yellow tape. The body has been outlined with white tape and the growing number of spectators is held at bay outside of the area. I hear the word *suicidarsi* (suicide).

What seems like the entire Florence police force is on the scene, standing, sitting on motorcycles, chat-ting, and smoking cigarettes. Mercifully, the body has been covered with a white sheet—now blood-stained, a mottled pink and red. A foot sticks out from under the sheet. I can't help noticing that the shoe appears new. There are no scuffmarks on the sole of the man's loafer. Florentines are elegant and always dress perfectly. Had this man bought new shoes for his death? There is an Italian expression that is popular among Florentines, *"Bella figura,"* which means making a good impression in the eyes of society. Perhaps this man did not want to die with old, worn shoes.

I guess the body has to be kept in place for investigation but it upsets me that the ambulance has come and gone but the body is still here.

We needed additional keys to the apartment and had to call Suzanne, who arrives on her motorino and takes us downstairs and across the street to *il calzolaio* (the cobbler) who also makes keys. He stands in the wood-framed doorway painted the color of Gulden's mustard, wearing a white lab coat covered with shoe polish. He had been one of the first spectators of this morning's event and nods recognition to me as we enter his tiny shop. *"Salve,"* he says.

I ask him how old the person was who died. He tells me the man was 80 and was sick. He was depressed and most likely on medication, he continues in Italian. He also mentions that he was wearing bulky clothing, like a bathrobe. I ask what was on his head and he tells me that the man had put a bag over his head.

"But he was wearing new shoes," I tell him. "Ah," the young cobbler says, as he looks down to make the key, *"ter-ri-bi-le."* The Italians pronounce every syllable and the word lasts a long time. He shakes his head back and forth; he had just resoled the shoes for the man the previous day, he says, sighing and somehow seeming to feel a sense of responsibility. "*Depressione,*" he exhales.

We leave the shop. "I was going to take my shoes there," my husband says. "I just changed my mind."

The newly cut key does not work. "How odd that you would notice the new shoes," our realtor says. "That is very observant." The day wears on and I continue to think of the man and his family. The body is finally gone but yellow tape remains on the street, marking his presence.

I start to think, what if I had left two minutes earlier? The guy would have landed on my head and taken me out with him. I'm not ready to go. I'm trying to get settled in the new place. I am annoyed that there are no salt and pepper shakers in the apartment and obsessing over the towels—so stiff -- and the mosquitoes are back full force. But a man was dead and he was left to lie in the street for hours. *Why did he put a bag over his head?* Maybe, so that he wouldn't see the ground he was hurtling toward. Or was he trying to asphyxiate himself simultaneously?

At eight o'clock in the evening we leave for dinner, and once again walk past the scene. The body outline tape is now gone, all that is left is some sandy substance that looks like kitty litter sprinkled over the remaining bodily fluids. As though it was not the remains of someone's life, but dog poop or spilled gelato.

I want to tell everyone who walks around it that a man died there hours earlier. But of course, I do not. I think of the inevitability of death that each of us will meet. Some people will have good and peaceful, timely deaths surrounded by loved ones. But this man chose a bad death, and I think of the desperation he must have felt. Oddly, I feel the need to grieve for a man I did not know.

I awake the next morning to the sound of the street-cleaning trucks and rush to the window. The powerful rotating brushes trudge slowly down Via dell' Oriuolo, erasing any sign of the previous day's drama, along with the cigarette butts and gelato cups and other carelessly discarded waste. I watch as the last cells of the unknown man are scrubbed away, and I think of how ephemeral and fragile life really is.

Once we were happily settled in our new home, Suzanne takes us out to dinner at Birreria Centrale at Piazza de'Cimatori. We were sitting outside on this delightful and relaxing evening, chatting and drinking wine, waiting for our food to arrive, when Florence's Elvis Presley impersonator walks into the square.

I have often seen him walking all over the city wearing his wig, outrageous rings, and white Elvis outfit. He sets up a speaker, strums his guitar and starts to sing, "Love Me Tender." Suzanne takes a gulp of wine, walks over to him, and says in her usual direct manner, "Who told you that you could sing? You are terrible; you can't even speak English; you're embarrassing yourself."

Elvis gets very upset, takes his guitar and leaves. An American at the next table says Suzanne upset him because he just came back from an Elvis contest in Memphis and thought he was doing great. Florence's abundance of tourists means that the sights are not all Michelangelo and Fra Angelico. There are also the Italian equivalents of Times Square's naked cowboy, and others.

Maestro is thrilled with his two new studio spaces. I am happy to have him around, and because of the size of the apartment, we don't get in each other's way.

We love our apartment, but there is no heat. Country law states that radiators stay off until November 1 in Florence, Rome, and certain other cities. Our heat is controlled by the building, not our individual unit. We are experiencing a recent drop in temperature but it is only mid-October. We are working all day, Bill painting, and me attempting to navigate blogs and a new website for *I Oprahed*.

One evening, we had planned to stay home for dinner, but by 6 p.m. we decided we need to get away from the chill. Bill is sitting in the living room with a coat, scarf, and hat. "It's too cold; we can't stay home for dinner."

We walk to Antica Sosta in Piazza Madonna degli Aldobrandini on the way to San Lorenzo market, but the bar has an open window and it is too cold for an *aperitivo,* so we continue on to Gilli in Piazza della Repubblica where the heat lamps are turned on for the outside seating.

Over our drinks, we discuss where to dine and decide we will try something totally new—an adventure. There is a place I often walk by named Marino at No. 8 Via della Oche, near the Paperback Book Exchange. I had peeked inside and it looked to be small, cozy and charming.

But all *trattorie* are not created equal—even in the mostly delicious city of Florence. It is still early, about 7:45, when we enter the inviting rustic room, which has about 12 tables. There are three men having dinner, the owner, the cook, and the waiter. We ask the waiter his name, and Leonardo shows us to a table. No other customers are present, nor do any materialize the entire time we are there—and for good reason.

We wait and wait while Leonardo stands in close proximity to the kitchen area, watching TV. Two children of the kitchen worker come in. One is a sulky female teen who sits on some steps that lead to living quarters upstairs, and the other is a boy of about 8 or 9 years who circles around the tiny restaurant with his hand-held video game—yelping as he leaps periodically from the kitchen's swinging door.

"So, how did you hear about this place?" my husband asks. I want to leave but finally Leonardo reappears. I ask if we may have some water and bread and tell him we want to order wine. He cannot take his eyes off the TV. I ask what is the pasta special of the day and what was fresh; he says, *"Io non so."* He doesn't know. He also doesn't care.

We sit. Fifteen minutes pass and some bread and water arrives. My husband orders lasagna. I request Milanese. Leonardo says *"E il pollo, non vitello"*—it is chicken, not veal. Half an hour passes and the food is delivered. The "Milanese," some kind of pressed and breaded mystery meat, obviously pre-frozen, is accompanied by three roasted potatoes. Not one time in the next 20 minutes does Leonardo come over to his only customers and ask how we are or how the food is. He stands 20 feet away watching TV, leaning on the wall. He clears our full plates, not seeming to notice the food is virtually untouched. This was without a doubt the worst food and worst service we've had in twelve years of Florentine dining.

My husband asks if I want to pick up a pizza or go someplace else. I do not. I will suffer in silence as my penance. As we are walking by L'Antico Noè, through the alley on Volta di San Piero, Massimo, the owner comes out to say hello. I weaken and ask if there is a table but of course they are totally booked, it is Friday night. He tells me he will give me some ravioli with ragu sauce *porta via,* to take away. So we go home, bundle up against the chill, and devour the delicious ravioli and wash it down with a delightful Villa Antinori Tuscan red. I've now been banned from future restaurant recommendations.

October is the month of the chestnut harvest and there are festivals all over Italy. In reading the current edition of *The Florentine*, the English-speaking news magazine in Florence, I see that the *Sagre delle Castagne* festival of chestnuts will take place on the coming weekend. There is an authentic vintage train, pulled by a steam-powered locomotive that will take us from Florence to Marradi, a mountain village located in the Tuscan Apennines, passing through Tuscany's countryside and several villages. It sounds wonderful and I can't wait to book it. The vintage coaches are sold out, but we can take the regular train instead. I have no trouble convincing my ever-enthusiastic husband; it's something we have never done—a once-in-a-lifetime opportunity to buy the famous Mugello chestnuts, chestnut flour and chestnut cake to take home.

This ends up on my "things *not* to- do" list. You probably will want to miss this event unless you would like to stand for an hour and a half squeezed into an old local train car with too many people, strollers, crying babies and shoving kids. If you really want chestnuts, you can buy them roasted all over the city, any time. I don't even like chestnuts but I seem to get caught up in the idea of a "festival" and think it's something I have to be a part of.

There was one positive, however: an old man roasting chestnuts over a fire who had a remarkable face showing years of life and toil. Bill asks to borrow my camera and takes several shots, which he uses to paint a very moving portrait of the man, whom we dubbed Paolo, at his studio.

After a day walking around the crowded streets and open markets, when we are more than ready to leave at around 5 p.m. we could not get on any of the scheduled trains back to Florence. There are hundreds of families with tired children pushing to the front of the platform. When the train stops, there is a stampede for the overflowing cars. Buses are ordered and they too fill up. We cannot figure out how to get back to Florence, so at 6 p.m. we return to Marradi and find a nice little restaurant for dinner. When we arrive back at the train platform after 9 in the evening, the trains departing are nearly empty. Maestro says I am now banned from choosing weekend events as well as new restaurants.

My favorite *gelateria* in Florence is also the oldest, Vivoli, on Via dell'Isola delle Stinche, near Santa Croce. For me Vivoli is a symbol of the city, just like the Duomo and *David*. There are so many stores all over the city selling gelato, but, without question, Vivoli is the best and most authentic.

One of my favorite flavors is *stracciatella,* or chocolate chip. The first time I went to Vivoli many years ago, with my limited Italian, I ordered a *schiacciata* (a classic Tuscan flat bread). The girl behind the counter laughed. *"Vuoi il pane?"* You want bread? Embarrassed, I made sure not to make the same mistake again.

Simonetta, the mother of the current owner in this third-generation family business, happens to be our neighbor now, in our building on Via d'Oriuolo. She is a lovely woman in her sixties who stands for hours at the cash register. This evening, we stop by for dessert and Bill gives her a *regallo* (gift); a striking print of one of his paintings of the Duomo, a scene he painted from our building. She is so thrilled that she comes from behind the counter and hugs him. *"Grazie, grazie,"* She then moves on to me, grabbing my face. *"Bacio, bacio"* (kiss, kiss). It is enough to bring me to tears. She insists on gifting us a giant cup of gelato. The framed painting still hangs on a wall of the world-renowned gelateria.

At Home in Florence

Perhaps one of the most significant improvements in the city since we began living here, can be attributed to Matteo Renzi, the city's young mayor, who was elected in June 2009. As one of Mr. Renzi's first moves in his new position, he turned the large square around Florence's Duomo into a pedestrian-only piazza. Without buses, taxis, and cars jamming the streets, it is now a thoroughly pleasant and totally new experience to walk around the magnificent cathedral and its Baptistry. This also means that our home is much more peaceful and quiet, since we live so close by.

One evening, we were invited to a dinner party at a friend's gorgeous apartment overlooking the Arno. She is a stunning Swedish woman who is married to an Italian-American. They live in Florence part time and they have a long-term lease on the "second best" apartment in the city. She is in a "mood" when we arrive because she just had gotten a terrible haircut, from a guy she went to last time she was in Florence who had given her the "best haircut of my life." "How could he have fucked up so badly today?" she asks.

The next morning I bump into my friend. She says she went to her lamp store today for the third time in two weeks to pick up new lampshades (the cleaning lady broke a lamp next to the bed, so they had to be replaced). "She told me to pick them up today at 4. Well, the girl in there looked surprised and still had no shades. What a pain. How do these people stay in business?" she asks. "Or maybe they don't."

I commiserate that it is always frustrating trying to get the most basic things done here. I've been waiting for three days for the "technician" to come and close my freezer door, which now resembles an igloo somewhere in the North Pole. This is the Italian way. Yet this year, when we leave for the spring art show and summer with the grandkids, we know where we will be coming back to in September. The inconveniences of life here are more than made up for by the delights.

When we return to "our" apartment in the fall of 2010 almost nothing has changed. The window boxes along the terrace have been filled with pink blossoming bougainvillea. There are new cushions on the stone built- in benches and chairs. We would be happy doing nothing but enjoying the atmosphere and pace of the city. In Sarasota, Bill has just completed a massive painting of an Alaskan glacier. He wants to take a few weeks off before deciding what to paint here.

But on our rooftop, witnessing the close up views of the Duomo, Baptistery, and Campanile, where you can almost reach out and touch the Duomo, his artistic inspiration strikes. He begins several paintings capturing different aspects of the Cattedrale di Santa Maria del Fiore. He says that when he went outside and set up several canvases and was ready to work and felt relaxed, a series of Duomo paintings emerged. "I hadn't planned this, but my hand took over."

His first painting becomes a large, simple painting of the top of the cupola with the cross. "When you let yourself go and let the environment take over, it's amazing what the result is," he says. He completes eight paintings in total, all quite different versions, and all buildings—not landscapes. The paintings are done at different times of the day: morning, afternoon, and a night scene that became a dramatic silhouette of the Duomo against the sunset. Bill says that sometimes the sunsets in Florence are equal to or even more beautiful than the sunsets on the Gulf of Mexico in Sarasota.

Our discovery for the best quick lunch near us is I Due Fratellini, a hole-in-the-wall restaurant located a few blocks from Piazza della Signoria on

Via dei Cimatori. Offering about 30 combinations of panini made with local Tuscan ingredients, served on a fresh crusty roll for a mere 2.50 euro, it is fast and delicious. We add a glass of basic red wine for Bill and basic white wine for me for an additional 2.50 each. Today we order soft goat cheese, Tuscan salami with fennel, and for Bill, fresh sausage with eggplant.

We stand around with the other patrons on the cobblestones of the narrow street out front, devouring our sandwiches. Here we can rest our glass of wine on a numbered slot on the wooden shelves flanking the doorway.

Despite our experience at the chestnut festival, we take the train to the tiny town of Figline Valdarno, located just 40 minutes from the heart of Florence, for our annual visit to the festival for the new oil and new wine. Every November Florentines anticipate the newly pressed, extra virgin, unfiltered olive oil -- green, spicy, and delicious. Here along the narrow cobblestone streets of the piazza you can taste fresh olive oil grown on the surrounding hillsides, talk to the family growers, and sample the region's famous wines.

Farmers, craftsmen, artists, and culinary artisans descend on the town, and some bring their animals with them—a proud farmer led his pair of prized white Chianina bulls, the enormous oxen native to Tuscany, through the crowd. The bustling streets are also filled with vendors of multi-colored fruits and vegetables and locally raised smoked meats and homemade pasta. Everywhere you look, there are samples being offered of meat, cheese, olive oil, and bread. The sights, sounds, and smells are dizzying and delectable.

Just outside of the town of Figline Valdarno, in the Chianti region, is where Sting and his wife, Trudy Styler, own a 900-acre estate known as Il Palagio. The villa was built in the 16th century and produces organic honey, wine, and olive oil. When we are leaving the festival, I have an idea: "Let's take a cab and see if we can find where Sting lives."

"What, are you nuts?" Bill says.

Despite his protests, he likes the idea, so we find a cab at the train station. *"Andiamo a casa Sting,"* I say. *"Sapete dove si trova?"* Do you know where it is? He nods his head up and down. *"Si."*

We get in the taxi and take off for a new adventure. *"Mi no piace Sting, ma mi piace Le Police."* He doesn't like Sting but he does like The Police, the driver says as he weaves his way through the countryside before arriving at the magnificent estate. There is no sighting of Sting or his wife. I think I read in the newspaper that they only come in the summer. There is a little shop on the property selling their organic production; we buy a bottle of the new oil and a jar of honey. Bill calls Brian Johnson in the States and asks him why he doesn't have an estate in Chianti.

Finished painting and writing, we have our fun week, which includes a family dinner with our friends at Buca Poldo, Christmas shopping, and saying *ci vediamo* and *arrivederci* to our friends. I decide to climb the 463 narrow stone steps to the top of the cupola of the Duomo, the only way to see the inside of the dome up close, and enjoy the extraordinary view of Florence. I can see our apartment from the top. I call Bill on my cell phone from outside when I reach the top; he goes out on our terrace and we wave to each other.

Hemingway and Stresa

In the fall of 2011, we had some friends visiting from the States around the time of our annual trip to Monteriggioni, San Gimignano, and Montalcino. We hire David Tweed for the day. As usual, our first stop is Monteriggioni, a tiny medieval walled town, built by the Sienese in 1214–19 as a front line in their wars against Florence. Following the mandatory stand-up cappuccino and brioche at the bar in the main square, we climb the stairs to the ramparts and walk along the wall.

Bill catches sight of a splendid vista of trees surrounded by houses and horses and takes numerous photos of the scene. Then on to Sienna, another lovely medieval city in Tuscany where we walk the site of the famous Palio horse race. We arrive in Montalcino ready for a wine tour and lunch. The next day, Maestro goes to Zecchi for supplies and starts to paint a 6x10-foot canvas in the downstairs studio. This unusual, complex painting is an overhead view looking down on the horses and the houses. He also paints a smaller version of the same scene.

It is a Sarasota connection that brings us to Stresa, a resort town of about 5,000 inhabitants on the shores of the Lago Maggiore, the second longest Italian lake, after Lake Garda in the region of Piedmont in northern Italy. But it is the ambiance and history of the commune that rekindles our love affair with Ernest Hemingway.

We take the morning train from Florence, change in Milan to a commuter rail for Stresa, where our friend Alessandro Rossi greets us as we cross the railroad tracks at the station. He drives us the five minutes to the elegant lakefront Hotel La Palma, situated in the center of town and surrounded by a garden, where he has booked a room for us. The spacious suite, with elegant classic décor, has a balcony that offers picturesque views of the Borromean Islands.

Alessandro is one of the owners of Mediterraneo, a top restaurant in Sarasota, Florida, that is among our favorites. But he was born and grew up in this peaceful upscale haven, where the main source of income is the tourist trade. His family runs a successful travel agency in Stresa, where he spends his time during their "season" when not working at the Sarasota eatery.

"I'm up here at Stresa, a little resort on Lake Maggiore, one of the most beautiful of the Italian Lakes." (E. Hemingway, 1929)

We are on a brief holiday, but something far more dramatic had brought a famous author to Stresa. In 1918, as war raged on in Europe, an 18-year-old Ernest Hemingway responded to a plea for ambulance drivers on the Italian front and left for Europe. In July of that same year he was seriously wounded while delivering cigarettes and chocolates to front line troops when a mortar exploded next to him. Despite the severity of his own wounds, Hemingway still managed to carry an Italian soldier to safety, for which he received the Italian Silver Medal of Bravery.

He spent the next six months recovering from the 227 shrapnel wounds to his legs in a Milan hospital. During this time Hemingway fell in love with Nurse Agnes von Kurowsky, whom he fictionalized as Nurse Catherine Barkley in *A Farewell to Arms* published many years later. Although it is a work of fiction, he had set part of his novel in Stresa. We want to follow his footsteps, so Bill downloads the novel to his Kindle and we begin reading.

We begin by taking the boat trip to Isola dei Pescatori (Island of the Fishermen), the small (population: 32) island famous for the charming simplicity of its old fishing village, which is considered one of the most picturesque spots on Lake Maggiore— and which was fictionalized in *A Farewell to Arms*. We walk along the cobbled alleys to the promenade that encircles the island and stop for a snack at Trattoria Imbarcadero before boarding the ferry for Isola Bella (Beautiful Island), a larger Borromean island.

On our final night, Alessandro and his gorgeous wife Valaria pick us up and drive along the shore road to the town of Lesa for an intimate lakeside dinner at Ristorante Il Rapanello, a seafood restaurant with stunning views of the lake. Alessandro orders an assortment of appetizers, followed by gnocchi with clams, ravioli of sea bass, and a variety of grilled fish.

We only stay a few days in Stresa, but promise ourselves we will return to this romantic getaway. After all, we read that Hemingway made numerous return visits.

October draws to a close. Several of our expat friends will be leaving in the next week and all want to get together with us prior to departing. We overschedule our week with nightly dinners, several of which turn into very late nights. *I Oprahed and Other Adventures of a Woman of a Certain Age,* my book of essays, has been released on Amazon, where the reviews and sales are respectable.

Bill's massive canvas of Monteriggioni is complete along, with several smaller canvases, and we head back to the States for Art Basel in Miami, followed by my official book signing and event in Sarasota and trips to Chapel Hill, North Carolina, and Boston to spend the holidays with our children and grandchildren.

La Vita Italiana

In 2012, we arrive at Pisa airport on a Sunday, but I am wondering how all five massive black suitcases with priority tags and attached red satin streamers did not make the plane connection in London. Bill suggests that the baggage handler must have been annoyed, since the bags were all very heavy. We are happy to see David Tweed, who is waiting with the oversized van to drive us to Florence—but we have no luggage.

My Italian LG cell phone does not work. We take a walk to the phone store and the clerk tells me I have to get a new number; it will work after midnight. I'm not sure why Bill's number is operational every year upon return, but mine never is, and we both use the same company.

We are happy that our home phone number is still the same but we are not happy that the ringer on the phone doesn't work.

We go to one of our favorite restaurants, L'Antico Noè, and run into our friend Shelby. There was a "nightmare" situation involving the pending sale of a condo and he and his wife are hiding out in a hotel. He is among the few ex-pats who own in Florence—but it might be simpler for him, since his wife is Florentine. He is telling Bill a long crisis-ridden story. We sit outside and have a delicious panini. Actually, I wait in line for 20 minutes for the food as Bill listens to Shelby's tale of woe. Massimo, the owner, gives us free wine, so we have to break our "no alcohol during the day" rule.

I am amazed that some women are riding by on bicycles in tank tops while others sport down vests and scarves wrapped around their neck. It's got to be 85 degrees. The Florentines invented the "layered look," and scarves are an essential accessory—they believe in keeping their necks warm at all times.

We go to back to the apartment to find there are still no bags. Since we flew on British Air, Bill thinks he will be connected to an English-speaking agent. He keeps saying *bags* to the occasional person he reaches by phone: "Press 1 for English." When he does as directed the response is, *"Pronto?"* *"Parla l'inglese?* Bill asks. "No." says the person. "What a surprise," he says. I tell him, "You must say *cinque valigie*---five suitcases."

On Monday a man from the delivery company calls at 5:30 in the evening and says that he will deliver our suitcases at 7:30. Even though he is only two blocks away, he says he can't come down our street until then; he needs a permit. Why would a delivery company need a permit to deliver something? Bill does not argue.

We've been in the same clothes for 53 hours; at least they're comfortable. British Air has given us a toiletry kit at my insistence, so we have toothbrushes. "Madame," the woman said at the lost baggage office at Pisa airport, "We will get you your luggage as soon as we can. It's only a day or two." In Italy, life is beautiful – just don't be in a hurry: *piano, piano.*

At exactly 7:30 that evening, the phone in the bedroom rings. The one in the living room is not working—I'm making a list for the handyman, Enrique. "Kelley!" a man yells into the phone, *"un minuto."* He is the courier. Bill is already waiting for him on the sidewalk outside of our building, prepared to wave him over and apologize to the impending backed-up traffic that will surely ensue. I am so tired I can't remember the word for husband—*il marito*—so I tell him *"lo sposato è di sotto"* (the married is downstairs).

Nevertheless, he delivers all five bags, which Bill has to drag into the building and up several stairs to the *ascensore* (elevator). I wait on the top floor to wheel them off—one at a time.

In case you haven't seen the elevators in Florence, they need describing. They are charming little wooden boxes measuring about 3 ½ by 3- by 7 feet high; as they go down on the pulleys, the weights go up—you can view the complete works through the window. It's a physics project.

Ours holds 3 or 4 small to medium-sized adults, or so the sign says—it's a tight fit. There is a metal door that opens out and then two doors that pull in flush to the box. All of these doors must be closed for the elevator to work. If you don't slam the metal door shut, the elevator does not function. This usually happens when I return from the market with twenty bags of food and have to walk up five flights of stairs. Elevators were an afterthought, put in a couple of centuries after the completion of the buildings. They squeeze them in wherever possible, usually behind a staircase.

Now that we have clean clothes, Bill picks up some painting supplies at Zecchi and reconnects with his friend Massimo, the owner. We take our first walk this fall to Mercato di Sant'Ambrogio for cheese, fruit, and olive oil, and then to the Mazzanti hardware store nearby in Piazza Lorenzo Ghiberti.

The sign says *mesticheria* (paintshop), *casalinghi* (housewares), and *ferramenta* (hardware). It is in an ancient building with creaky wooden floors and rooms going off in every direction, including downstairs. It appears that there is nothing they don't sell, except possibly cars and food.

Although it is packed and we have to take a number and wait, Bill insists on buying me my first ever shopping trolley—100 percent aluminum, "the Cadillac of carts," the tag says in English. Finally, I do not have to carry 12 plastic bags full of food the many blocks home from the market. It makes me feel old—the old lady with the shopping cart. Still, it's a great convenience.

It's raining—unusual for Florence in September. The manager of our apartment said they had fixed the leak from last year. But it's still leaking and I put a pan under the spot to catch the drippings, which are now pouring through the three light fixtures in the hallway ceiling. Never mind, it is still the best apartment in Florence.

Now officially unpacked, I'm not sure how I ended up with 24 pair of pants. Okay, five are yoga/sweatpants but 15 are black, of varying lengths, widths, sizes, and percentage of spandex. My most neurotic buy was two pairs of identical pants of khaki color that are so comfortable and that I love so much that the thought of the ruination of them with spilled red wine or olive oil spurred me to buy the second pair when they went on sale.

A few weeks ago the *Wall Street Journal* ran a story called "The Summer Staple with Legs." It was about white jeans sticking around for fall and winter, instead of being packed up at summer's end. Naturally, as a "fashion forward consumer," I packed my one and only pair of white jeans. The article said there was "something slightly rebellious about wearing white jeans in cold weather—breaking the traditional ban on white clothes after Labor Day."

Although I've been told in America that many dry cleaning machines are manufactured in Italy, the cleaning outcome differs greatly here. One is always at risk when leaving garments at the local *tintoria*-- the process of dry cleaning is *lavaggio a secco*.

"They shrink and they stink," my Italian friend says. I've tried at least half a dozen cleaners in Florence and have asked just about everyone I meet who they use, and everyone has similar horror stories of the designer pants that were ruined or returned two sizes smaller.

The most apparent missing step in the Italian process is adding sizing to the clothing. You drop off a perfectly good pair of pants with some life to them and they are returned like a limp handkerchief.

I try to avoid using the cleaners at all cost. The other problem is, everything takes at least a week in Florence. Italians have a word that covers all such situations, "*paziena*," patience.

I drop off a pair of Bill's pants Monday and they tell me to come back *Mercoledi,* Wednesday. I return two days later to pick them up and the woman tells me *proximo Mercoledi*—next Wednesday. Most recently I went to retrieve a pair of my khaki cotton slacks. I left them because I figured, *how they possibly ruin them?* At least they could get the olive oil stain out so it wouldn't have a chance to set. There was a pink circle the size of an Oreo cookie on the front; "ruined," Alma, the owner says. She thought it was an ink mark and tried to get it out but the fabric turned pink. She wanted to know if she should dye the pants pink. I'm kind of a classic dresser and pink pants were not going to work for me, particularly in Florence. I have heard, however, they do a good job with silk. After all, Florentines have been wearing silk since the Renaissance, but I'm not going to risk it.

Bill knows what he wants to paint this year for his large canvas. It's an idea he's had in the back of his mind for several years; he calls it *Autumn All Around the World.* It will be a group of colorful trees from our travels, including oak and maple trees from our former house in New Hampshire and cypress trees from China in the West Lake area of Hangzhou, which we found identical to the cypress trees in Tuscany; they also serve the same purpose—the delineation of property. There is a lime tree from Fiesole, and lime trees from Provence and a group of olive trees from Tuscany.

It takes most of the fall to complete this canvas. When Sister Wendy sees the photo of the painting, she calls it, "Trees from heaven." On the top floor, in the *piccionaia*, the large room off the roof with skylights, Bill produces several more paintings, the most significant of which is a scene of three olive trees—the concept germinates from the large tree painting he is working on. One of the trees is identical to the one in the foreground of the grand painting-- silver blue along with a pink and a white. He names it, *Tre Alberi di Ulivo*- three olive trees.

One of the things I love about Bill having his studios in our apartment is that when he finishes up at around 6 p.m. each day, he emerges from the elevator on the main floor and gets off with only his shoes and underwear on. He carries his clothes to the laundry rolled up under his arm as he walks to the shower. "Honey, I'm home," he announces. This gives me notice to change and get ready for dinner.

One evening, we are having dinner with our expat friend Mary, who is married to Mario, a handsome and charming Florentine. We meet at Trattoria 13 Gobbi on Via del Porcellana, directly across the street from where they live. Because the owner knows Mario, we are seated at the best table and given a significant *sconto,* discount. This is a great perk in Florence. If you frequent an establishment and pay cash, the owner will often give a reduction on the bill. We walk home and, just as I suspected would happen, there was olive oil on my tan pants. Fortunately I have the replacement. Good thing I didn't wear my white jeans.

Thirteen years ago Mary was traveling around Italy with a group of friends. She was single—never married, no children and 45 years old at the time. One evening in Florence, when the group scattered (two to the gay bar behind Rivore), she returned to her hotel, The Excelsior, and headed to the bar, alone, for a nightcap. There she met the handsome recent widower and bar manager of the five-star hotel. They talked until the wee hours. He called her every day when she returned to the States and visited her numerous times the first year. She gave up her advertising business in Connecticut and moved to Florence. The moment I met Mary, I knew we would be pals. Mary Agnes, Catholic schooled, just like me.

I wake up with a scratchy throat the next day, but am enticed away from the computer to have lunch with Mary at the Gucci museum restaurant in Piazza della Signoria. There have been a few Bill Clinton sightings in the city, and who knows, we may run into him; I always bring a camera.

I arrive first, just after 1. It is a splendid sunny day as I approach the waitress. *"Tavolo per due—per pranza, per favore."* You get the point. She looks at me and in Italian says that it is not possible, they are totally booked, but maybe inside there is availability. I stand looking at the vacant tables. *Were they reserved? Did they only want Italians outside? I'll wait for Mary; she speaks perfect Italian and is quite friendly and demonstrative.*

I spot Mary coming across the piazza wearing black leggings and a thigh-length fashionable black sweater, looking Italian-chic. I tell her the situation. She inquires how I asked for the table. "Hmmm," she says, after I tell her what I said. Suddenly, her chic outfit becomes a nun's habit and she is looking like Sister Mary Agnes.

She approaches the same waitress and in an extraordinarily friendly manner says that we want a table for two on the terrace—exactly the way I had said it. "Si Signora, un minuto," the very same woman says to Mary. Perhaps it was Mary's accent that got us a table, but I think it was more likely her clothes.

We do not need to stay for a four-hour lunch and drink a few glasses of wine each—but we do anyway. Besides, the service is so slow that we had to do something while we waited. After sitting for over an hour, the waitress approaches and tells Mary that what she ordered—a couscous salad—is "finished." When did that happen? And why couldn't we know sooner? The Italians will never tell you that they ran out of something; that would put the onus on them. Saying that something is finished leaves it up in the air, like it just happened and they had no control over it.

Settling In

I t's the end of September when we see in the paper that Iggy Pop is playing at 7:30 tonight in Piazza della Repubblica, one of the main squares in Florence. One of the surrounding bars, Caffé delle Giubbe Rosse (so-called because of the red jackets of the waiters) was a meeting point for many of the city's artists and writers in the past; Bill and I try to stop in every now and then for an *aperitivo* to soak up the atmosphere of past greatness and creativity.

We're going to Cammillo for dinner, which is on the other side of the river, but we have to walk through the Piazza della Republica to get there. I don't know who Iggy is, and it's raining. I can imagine masses of young people with beer bottles trying to get a glimpse of the musician on the newly erected outside stage. I Google "Iggy Pop" and read that he is the leader of punk rock groups and performs naked from the waist up. We decide to walk to the Piazza, have a glass of wine, and check out the scene on the way to dinner. It's wild and crazy with thousands of young people elbow to elbow, some on each other's shoulders chanting, "Iggy, Iggy." AC/DC we love. Iggy Pop, not so much.

It is the last Sunday in September and today is the day of the annual Corri la Vita (Run for Life), a 13-kilometer competitive race and 5-kilometer non-competitive walk for charity that supports public health facilities specializing in the fight against breast cancer. Today it begins in Piazza Duomo. Bill buys the T- shirts now provided by Ferragamo—royal blue, this year—and registers us for the race. This is a tradition and a cause we are devoted to--but I have come down with a deadly cold so I am forced to opt out. It's early in the season to be sick, but the alternating heat and humidity, rain, dampness and cold of the morning and evenings, coupled with the germs at the Supermercato on the cart handles, ganged up on me, leaving me a sniveling, sneezing, headachy mess.

Corri la Vita has reached the 10th year, and the organizers, headed by several women members of the Frescobaldi family, have chosen to celebrate this milestone by involving the city of Florence and all important places of interest. The run and the walk will take walkers through many palaces and gardens and past monuments and museums. It is always a day we look forward to. But I can't get out of bed. I always use my Purel hand sanitizer after shaking hands and keep it in my purse. I especially love the people who come up and insist on kissing me on the mouth and then tell me they have a really bad flu.

I'm reading *The Stones of Florence* in my illness and Mary McCarthy didn't exactly love Florence. I am declaring myself cured tomorrow. I'm too ADD to sit and read all day. Following the 5k walk, my compassionate husband calls and asks how I'm doing. He tells me he ran into just about everyone we know in Florence at the walk today. "Is it okay if I go to lunch with a group afterward as we always do?" he asks. I say, "Sure," but I mean, *How can you possibly be having so much fun without me? Don't you want to come home and feed me chicken soup?*

Bill never gets sick. He takes three drops of pure oil of oregano in a spoonful of olive oil daily. Occasionally, he takes a Zinc-C herbal lozenge.

I remember that there is nothing with red dye in Italy—meaning no Nyquil. I forgot to bring mine, so I sneezed and coughed myself to sleep last night. The pharmacist does have Vicks green liquid for night. He says it's like the real thing. Today I am on a hunt for lemons *limone,* easy enough, honey, *miele,* and cloves. Some words in Italian are way too complicated, like cloves—*chiodi di garofano.* Some people say cloves in heated red wine will get rid of *il raffreddore.*

Wednesday is Day Four of the cold and all the Mucinex D is "finished." After lunch, I do my first walk outside and find myself at Max Mara on Via Tournabouni in the center of Florence. The building itself is stunning, the clothes are chic, and good value, and there are frescoes on the walls. But salespeople all over Florence have a habit of stalking, so my response, *sto solo cercando* (I'm just looking) doesn't work for them. One particularly close follower today has terrible cigarette breath. Have I mentioned that just about everyone smokes in Florence?

It's October and Bill has been working on his massive, 6x10-foot canvas, *Autunno in Tutto il Mondo,* in the downstairs studio. He has been painting the bottom of the canvas on his hands and knees for the past two days and is tired. He wants to go to Fiesole to relax and have lunch with Francesco at his wonderful restaurant, Etrusca. We discovered this family run restaurant many years ago and often come on Saturday or Sunday. The food is excellent and they have a wood burning oven which delivers excellent pizza. Francesco generally sits with us on the outside terrace and then he doesn't charge us for most of our meal.

Bill insists over lunch that he thought it might have been better in the old days when we had to go to Internet cafés to get online. Until the last five years, no apartments had WiFi in Florence. We had to go to an Internet café or the Internet Train to check emails. Why they were called that remains a mystery; they were neither cafés nor were they motorized. Usually they were filled with hung-over students with the flu who hogged the computers and sneezed on them between bites of a panini. They were great places to pick up a cold. Having a personal WiFi at home now is a huge step forward. But his point is well taken. We spend too much time on the computers in Florence now because of the accessibility, just like everywhere else.

Dejan, Bill's former studio mate, has asked us to attend his art show. There is an exhibition of local artists in what is the newly restored and reopened Santo Stefano al Ponte in collaborazione con Artis Florence e con il Patrocinio del Comune di Firenze, a side street between the Ponte Vecchio and Piazza della Signoria. We do not know there is an admission charge and Bill has only 50 euro notes, having just come from the bank. There is a long line and some people are apparently buying 2 euro tickets to the show, while others try to purchase a more expensive ticket, which includes an *aperitivo* and snacks, but we are unable to find out the amount. The man behind the glass taking the money does not have change. Every entry necessitates his leaving the booth and going somewhere for change, and the entry line grows longer and longer. There is much writing on tickets and stamping of documents, which takes an inordinate amount of time. We finally find one euro when Dejan appears, and we have to borrow 3 euros from him to get into his show. Italian bureaucracy is omnipresent and surely must be partly responsible for Italy's financial troubles.

———∞∞∞———

Our first houseguests this year are my younger brother, Blaine, and his six-foot-tall stunning blonde wife, Kellie. On the Friday when they arrive, I go to Saint Ambrosia market in the morning and buy fresh Tuscan bread, olive oil, prosciutto, and cheese for lunch. At the cheese market I buy buffalo mozzarella for a Caprese salad, along with some fresh basil and two gorgeous tomatoes at the vegetable stand.

On Saturday I have made reservations for them at the museums, Uffizi at 11 a.m. and the Academia at 2 p.m. It's a lot to take in in a short amount of time, but they won't be in Florence long. I tell them these and the Duomo are the "must sees" of Florence. The restored original *David* at the Accademia, Bill tells them, is the most famous piece of art in the world. I am hoping they won't be too tired with their nine-hour time difference. But my brother is 10 years younger than I, and his wife an additional seven years younger. They have youthful energy, and off they go. It's a treat for me to have a family member visit and be able to show them the places we love.

On Sunday we walk down our street, through Volta di S.Piero archway, past Santa Croce, across the Ponte alle Grazie and through the village of San Niccolò. We are on our favorite Sunday hike up the stone steps to Piazzale Michelangelo-- a serious walk. Here at the top are beautiful views over the rooftops of Florence, as well as a copy of Michelangelo's *David*.

We have a stand-up cappuccino at the bar. We stroll along Viale Gallileo to San Leonardo and turn right on this narrow, snaking, one-way street leading back down to the Arno and the Ponte Vecchio. Cars fly by with flagrant disregard for pedestrians. We slam our bodies up against the stone wall to avoid sudden death as a red Ferrari rounds the tight corner at record speed.

As we approach a small church along the walk, Church of S. Leonardo in Arcetri, my brother pushes the gate open and walks into the courtyard to take a photo. It slams behind him. He is unable to hide his panic when he realizes he is locked in behind a high spiked fence.

"I don't think I can climb that," he says anxiously. Ironically, the church, built in the 11th century, is dedicated to the French patron saint of prisoners. Once again, as in his youth, he is a prisoner of the Catholic Church.

Kellie and I are peeking through the bars of the gate at my brother on the other side, laughing uproariously, which infuriates him. Like a caged lion he paces, then tries the door of the church. Locked. He spots an arched doorway to the right of the church. There is a button with a plastic cover, which he presses on and off. It's a light. To the left of the door is what looks like a bell. I tell him to ring the bell. With any luck, the priest lives there. Minutes pass and a man of the cloth appears, looking rather exasperated.

Blaine tells him in Spanish that he has locked himself in the courtyard. The priest listens and seems to comprehend, then nods. He closes the door and returns a few minutes later with a giant ring of keys. *"Grazie, Padre,"* I tell him. *"Me dispiache, per la rottura."* I'm sorry for the disruption. He is now smiling and asks, *"È questo suo marito?"* And this is your husband? I tell him he is my brother, but that my husband is over there hiding. He gives a hearty laugh as we go on our way, waving goodbye and wishing him a happy Sunday. *"Buona domenica."*

We walk past Forte di Belvedere, a rambling fortress designed by Bernardo Buontalenti for Grand Duke Ferdinando I at the end of the 16th century, eventually ending up on Costa dei Magnoli, a steep, narrow street lined with bright yellow stone houses which spills out on to the Via de Bardi in front of The Golden View Bar, a favorite restaurant of ours. We have a wonderful lunch, while Sasha, our preferred waiter, entertains us, so we have many laughs.

Blaine and Kellie take off for Venice for a few days and when they return we book our friend and driver, David, for a day in central Tuscany. The weather is gorgeous as we meet up in front of the Savoy hotel and head off once again to the medieval hilltop town of Monteriggioni. We climb up to the top of the walls for spectacular views of the surrounding countryside (which Bill has painted so brilliantly) from the walkway. Dante is said to have written his *Inferno* in the town.

Our next stop has a Sarasota connection. Casali di Bibbiano is owned by Alberto Guadagnini, who is the proprietor of Salute Restaurant, near where we live in Florida. It is a recently restored 18th-century country estate and winery on 85 acres of land including vineyards, olive groves, and luxury villas. It operates as a full-production winery of award-winning super Tuscan wines, including Cabernet Sauvignon, Merlot and Sangiovese. Additionally, high-quality olive oil is pressed from the olive trees growing on the country estate, which Alberto imports to use at Saluté. Our guides, Davide and Claudia graciously describe the progress of the grape from the vine to the vineyard barrel as they give us a tour. My brother, who lives in Yakima, Washington, has recently planted several acres of grapes for wine making, so he is especially intent.

We have a tasting in their gorgeous kitchen overlooking the rolling hills and olive groves and buy a case of Super Tuscan wine, the premium wine of the region that has become sought after by wine connoisseurs worldwide, promising to return. It's a quiet day here, as this is considered the end of the season. The handsome and charming chef tells me that he offers Italian cooking classes to visiting groups. He points out the vegetable and herb garden right outside the restaurant. While he talks with us, he is grilling thin slices of eggplant, red pepper and zucchini all freshly picked. My brother and I agree this beautiful spot with its elegant hotel would be spectacular for a family reunion. The restored villas can accommodate 26 people—an extraordinary venue. There is a gym, tennis and basketball courts, and a gorgeous swimming pool with a Jacuzzi. And the staff is fluent in English, as well as Italian.

Next, we visit Montalcino, whose foremost activity is wine producing. The highest point is the 14th century Fortezza, a fortress, with a wine shop in the walls, where the magnificent local Brunello wines are for sale. We stop to sample the wines before dining at Osteria di Porta al Cassero on Via della Libertá, filled with locals. A two-minute walk from the Fortezza, the restaurant features homemade pastas and soups, grilled sausages, potato and meat croquettes, stewed wild boar served with the tiny, creamy white Tuscan beans, and all washed down with an excellent Brunello. On their final night, our generous houseguests take us to Cammillo Trattoria for a farewell dinner, where we have another classic Tuscan meal.

They must leave at 5:30 in the morning for the airport in Pisa. We order the taxi the night before, but I set my alarm for five, just to be sure. We call again in the morning and tell them the address, and after one minute on hold the operator comes back. "*Quattro minuti.*" Sure enough, in exactly four minutes, the taxi arrives. Taxi service in Florence is one thing that runs on time.

I turn on the computer this morning and open an email from my friend Sally; she is *on* for lunch today and hopes we can make it to Alimentari Perini at Mercato Centrale at 1 p.m. She entices me by saying she wants to introduce us to Andrea, the owner, who also does catering for their parties. A caterer has always been a missing part of my Florence team. If we have even a small dinner party, I find myself making too many trips to the market, cooking, *and* being the server. Bill wants to come along.

It's a very cold damp day in the 40s with intermittent rain, as Bill and I walk to Mercato Centrale, the massive indoor food market at San Lorenzo located in a towering cast-iron building dating from 1874.

Andrea, the owner-- tall, handsome and smiling comes from behind the counter as we enter and greets us with big hugs. He leads us across the aisle to a glass partition with a stand-up counter just inside the market main door and pops open a bottle of Prosecco, the Italian version of champagne. Goblets appear in seconds, along with a platter of prosciutto, salami, and hard, aged cheese with little drops of fig jam dotted on top of each piece. The feast continues with a vast array of Tuscan delicacies, including crostini, delicious pecorino cheese with pear preserves, and chunks of Parmigiano-Reggiano. A folded-down brown paper bag filled with cut-up pieces of warm, freshly baked, crusty bread arrives, accompanied by a dish of the coveted new green, unfiltered, spicy olive oil—the new production of 2012. When the Prosecco is finished, Iwona, the tall, good-looking, blonde fiancée of Andrea, arrives with a bottle of Chianti. All this takes place in the bustling atmosphere of this grand indoor market, which is replete with butcher shops selling every part of just about every animal, from pig's feet to whole chickens with their heads and feet still attached, and beef tripe, the white, rubbery looking lining of a cow's stomach. There's a seafood area, with several vendors featuring fish and shellfish of all kinds, cheese shops, and stalls selling pasta. And there are gorgeous vegetables from Italy as well as the rest of the Common Market.

We must be the envy of all the passersby who enter the market, staring at us eating and drinking with obvious enjoyment. The other employees of Perini come and chat with us as we stand beneath the hanging legs of prosciutto and ropes of garlic surrounded by giant wheels of Parmigiano and jars of jams and honey. Although the market closes at 2pm, we stay on, honored guests, among the few people left in the cold, massive concrete space with its now-empty stalls.

Because Sally and Joe are leaving in a couple of days on a ship that will cross the Atlantic from Civitavecchia, the port of Rome, today, they want to say goodbye to all of their merchant friends. They invite us to accompany them on all their stops.

At 4 o'clock we head to the Trattoria Centrale for a quick goodbye, and then to Tony Sasa at Enoteca Ponte Vecchio—the wine shop. He is in the middle of a lecture and wine tasting with a group of about 20 Europeans. He uncorks a bottle and pours us each a taste of red. "No, grazie," I say. "What, you don't drink wine?" He sounds offended. Oh, yes, I do, it's just that we have some English friends and Francesco from Fiesole coming at five o'clock to our house for drinks and to view the new "masterpiece" that Bill has been working on. We've also been tasting wine since one o'clock. I discover Tony will deliver, so make a mental note to add him to the purveyors I can call on in the future.

After a brief stop, we head home and stop to buy a lime from Rosa at the produce stand in the square by our house. The English couple drinks gin and tonics with lime. As we approach our door, we see two people standing in front. Our guests are early; it's 4:50pm. They have two bottles of Poggio Antico 2003

Riserva Brunello di Montalcino that they have just brought back from the vineyard. Francesco is close behind. We set out some recently purchased cheese, bread, and salami and pour the Brunello.

The following morning I wake up and the first thing I think is that all the visitors are *gone*. I roll over and go back to sleep.

Massage with Maximilliano

My neck and back are in chronic pain from writing hunched over my laptop computer. Bill is aching from working on his large canvas, as well as five smaller ones. We are both feeling exhausted from late nights and working days. I suggest we schedule Lisa's massage therapist, Maximilliano, a Thailand-trained therapist who works with the ballerinas at Florence Dance.

A few years ago, when I suffered similar neck issues, I had him come to the apartment. But this is not a therapist who brings a professional massage table with him. In the past, he arrived on his *motorino*, a handsome man of about 40 with a big smile. I lay on my stomach on the bed, practically fully clothed, but with my shirt off and bra on as Max did some form of Thai deep tissue work on my sore muscles. Bill kept walking by and looking in, horrified. It was the least relaxing experience imaginable, and, in fact, caused more tension.

"I never thought I'd see my wife lying naked with another man rubbing her," Bill had said when Max left. I'm still not sure why I didn't ask Max to close the door, but perhaps I felt safer with a strange man knowing that Bill was close by. In any case, for the next few years I did not call Max; it was easier to suffer. But I have an idea that if we both use him, Bill will most likely become friends with him, so I schedule massages for the two of us. Sure enough, there is an instant connection. They compare notes on Thailand, where they both spent time, Max studying massage and Bill painting many canvases before I met him. The next day Bill emails photos of his Thailand paintings to Max. They are now buddies. I feel better and so does Bill. I can now look forward to having guilt-free massages in the future.

<hr />

November 10, and I am now in the panic mode, as we have less than a month left here. We left Florida eight weeks ago today, and the time has flown by at record speed. We decide to treat ourselves to dinner at Cammillo Trattoria Thursday night. This is without question the best Tuscan food in Florence I spotted the Barefoot Contessa, Ina Garten, there last year.

Today is Saturday and as Bill reminds me, we only have two more Saturdays this year in Florence. Tomorrow the forecast is for a 100 percent chance of rain. I plan to stay home all day, so I need to buy some food. I manage to coerce Bill into walking with me *to*

Mercato di Sant'Ambrogio. Although I have passed this way hundreds of times, as we reach the piazza, I notice that the doors are open at Sant'Ambrogio, a church allegedly built where Saint Ambrose stayed in Florence in 393. The first building on the site is thought to date from the 8th century, a chapel that was part of a convent built in honor of the saint. Francesco Granacci (1469–1543), an Italian painter of the Renaissance and lifelong friend of Michelangelo Buonarroti, is buried in this church. We enter and marvel at the numerous frescos, altarpieces, and other artwork attributed to Masaccio, Filippo Lippi, Sandro Botticelli, Fra Bartolomeo, and many other artists.

Now we are off to the market and the *macelleria* (butcher), where, if you have a brain, you stay away from on Saturday. Every woman in the neighborhood is buying her meat for the next week and no one is in a hurry when her turn comes. I take a number: 05. They are currently on number 75. Bill looks at me. "I thought you never came here on Saturday." Well, I didn't get here yesterday, so here we are. Forty-five minutes later, Luca and Sandro are only up to number 97 (with two extra people working), where they stay for another 20 minutes. It is during this time that Bill leaves to buy paint brushes at Zecchi, his art supplier, and promises to call me on his way home to meet up for cappuccino. I finally get my meat and fresh eggs (the date stamped on each one) and tell Sandro I will see him next week to order my *tacino* (turkey) for Thanksgiving. There's a big *festa* in Piazza Republica this weekend and I head there to buy some of the new olive oil, peppery and deeply green.

Chiara and Massimo show up at 11:30 in the morning to view the massive landscape of the Maestro. It is pouring rain—*"tempo e bruto,"* Chiara says as she shakes out her umbrella. What fun to have them here. They love Bill's work and want to order a garden scene from Bill's website for their bedroom. *"Sono un giardiniere* (I am a gardener),"* Massimo says. Florentines buying Tuscan artwork by an American painter is very flattering.

Tonight we have Mary and her husband Mario coming over for drinks and a viewing of this year's collection of paintings and then on to Trattoria Armando on Borgo Ognissanti. We take the long walk from our house past the Excelsior Hotel to the restaurant, where Bill always gets spaghetti alla carretiera followed by *polpettine di vitella*, veal meatballs which are lemony and light. I love the home made ravioli with ricotta and radicchio. Mario and Mary order fried artichokes and fagioli (fresh white beans) with olive oil and sage and we order extra antipasti for the table. Mario and the owner worked together at the Splendido in Portofino when they were young.

The next night we go out for dinner but are home early; just soup and a pizza at Baldavino in Santa Croce. We didn't need to stop at Vivoli for gelato on the way home but we do anyway.

It must be time to go back to the States because Bill has started to refer to himself in the third person as "Maestro." I ask him to move a heavy chair and he replies, "Maestro can't do that now. It's not on his schedule." Good thing I love him.

The Art of Shoes

Mary and I go to the Ferragamo Museum on the Friday after Thanksgiving, situated in the basement of Palazzo Spini Feroni on Via Tornabuoni, to see the Marilyn Monroe exhibit. It is to honor the 50th anniversary of her death in August of 1962. This is something I think Bill would not be interested in, but when we arrive, I realize he would love it.

The first room is a display of Salvatore Ferragamo's shoes from years past. These are works of art and so stunning that every pair would be perfect for today's fashion. Behind the glass is a pair of stacked and layered colorful platforms made for Judy Garland in 1938. Lady Gaga would kill for these today. The collection includes platform suede booties from 1938-39, cork platforms, wedge booties, woven sandals, and pumps -- all stunning. There are also wooden shoe models with names of famous stars like Sophia Loren, Greta Garbo, Audrey Hepburn, stenciled on the side and prototypes.

Both Salvatore Ferragamo and Marilyn Monroe are timeless icons of their era; neither will ever go out of style. Along with the Bert Stern and Milton

Green photos surrounding the walls, video screens display clips from her movies. There is one theatre-size room devoted to Marilyn's costumes and dresses from films. They look small, but I remember reading she was a size 12. The focal point is a massive screen in the center of the stage playing film clips in which Marilyn is wearing the dresses on display.

In a long display case against the wall are 26 pairs of identical pumps, size 7 ½, in varying colors but mostly neutral tones—beige to gold to camel to taupe. All were well-worn by Marilyn. Then comes a large display of bright red dresses and red rhinestone-studded pumps looking not unlike the ruby slippers from *The Wizard of Oz*.

We are now running out of time as six o'clock approaches and the security guard advises us to speed it up. But we are mesmerized by the many photos of Marilyn at every stage in her life, in every production. Her words and actual notebooks are displayed, along with the poetry she wrote.

Nearing the end of the exhibition is a copy of the dress Marilyn wore to sing happy birthday to President Kennedy in 1962, and another screen replaying Peter Lawford's introduction of Marilyn, after which she takes the microphone and breathily sings, "Happy birthday, Mr. President."

At the very end we are ushered out past a large white room with a bed and what looks to be a white sheet covering a body; there is a big photo of Marilyn on the wall in the center. The notation is the year and time she died, and the drugs that were in her system at the time of her death. What an upsetting end to what seemed a light-hearted look at the screen legend's footwear.

It's hard to leave on such a shocking note. I want to go back to the beginning and start all over, but it will have to be on another day. *"Il museo è chiuso,"* the guard tells us. Mary and I head to the St. Regis for an *aperitivo* and to discuss the exhibit. As we leave we are feeling stunned and speechless.

Maestro has just announced that he is finished with his painting for the year. It is November 17, the next-to-last Saturday before we leave, and it is a beautiful and sunny day. Mary bought me a package of Tulip brand bacon—a rare commodity in Florence. I'm doing an American breakfast of eggs, bacon, and toast, which we will eat outside on the terrace. Then we will go to Mass at the Duomo and after that, take a taxi up to Fiesole to bid farewell to Francesco.

It was my idea to attend Mass at the Cathedrale di S. Maria del Fiore even though we are fallen away Catholics. There is a five o'clock in English—I checked the schedule—so off we go. There are two priests who almost speak English, one from India, near Calcutta, and one from Egypt. They are passing through Florence like so many of us, one of them explains. There is much talk about being forgiven for our sins. The concept of sin, so central to Catholicism is certainly one of the reasons I no longer consider myself Catholic.

The ceremony has changed since I grew up, when the Mass was shrouded in the mystery of incense and delivered in Latin. At the end, the priest suggests we all give a handshake of peace to those surrounding us. Good thing I brought my Purel hand sanitizer. Some participants lift their hands upward as though they are witnessing a miracle as they recite the "Our Father" prayer. When the service is over, we exit rapidly out the side door and take a cab to Fiesole, happy to be released.

We meet Francesco at the JJ Hill Pub for what has now become a standard *aperitivo*. Once again, like every year, he tells us he will not be here when we return next fall as he has a new interested buyer. Bill smiles, wishes him well, and pays no attention.

We cross the street to his restaurant and are greeted by Mohammad, the Egyptian pizza maker who has worked there for 17 years. He makes the best pizza in Florence. He delivers a basket of focaccia bread, which is paper thin and crispy and drizzled with olive oil and tomato sauce, followed by the most delicious veal pizziola. When I ask for the recipe, Francesco says his cook sautés the tender veal in butter and tops it with fresh tomato sauce and a few capers.

For the spaghetti, garlic is sautéed in olive oil, then sprinkled with a little pepperoncini and topped with fresh parsley, then the cooked pasta is added and tossed. Fresh is the key word here. I'm just happy we don't have a scale in Florence. It could be depressing. We hug Francesco goodbye and take the number 7 bus back to Florence.

The next week, we leave to see our family in North Carolina and Boston. We plan to return the following fall.

Florence in the Fall

The best time to come to Florence is the early fall, when the summer crowds have abated and it is nearing harvest time for olives and grapes. These days, we arrive in September and stay till mid-December. Bill refuses to leave until after December 8, the *Fierucola dell' Immacolata*, Feast of the Immaculate Conception. On this day, the Catholic faithful celebrate the conception of the Virgin Mary free of Original sin. It's not the religious aspect—lapsed Catholics that we are—as much as the excitement of this national holiday that we eagerly anticipate. The chill is in the air; it's the official beginning of the Christmas season and the streets are bustling with happy shoppers. Decorative lights illuminate the city, and the lights on the massive tree in front of the Duomo are ceremoniously turned on to loud cheers and a speech by the mayor.

Leslie, the manager of our building greets us as we arrive, in the late afternoon. The apartment looks beautiful. I notice two new lampshades in the living room, and there are new wooden dining chairs that will take some getting used to. They are quite uncomfortable. We see that our pillows and various other things we stored when we left last December -- the blender for morning smoothies, the mattress cover, Bill's easel and paintbrushes – are back in the places where we left them. We look at the Duomo, take a deep breath, exhale, and quietly rejoice at being back.

As the evening approaches, we walk to Caffè Rivoire, in Piazza della Signoria for an *aperitivo*. Salvatore appears in his starched white shirt, black vest and pants—the summer uniform. He greets us effusively and then all the waiters circle around us, delivering hugs and kisses. *"Maestro, come stai? Senora Susanna, ciao—troppo elegante. Tutto bene?"* Bill looks at me and smiles; life is good and the WiFi works at home. *Bravo!*

We've been juicing for breakfast for the past nine months. We're not zealots but we feel healthier—at least that's what we keep telling ourselves. Bill has lost 20 pounds, because he has also given up bread and because men can always lose weight easily. I am the same weight. We are determined to continue the practice but it's impractical to pack the massive, heavy Breville juicer. I buy a small NutriBullet at Macy's and bring it with us.

We spend the first week settling in, visiting our favorite restaurants, catching up on sleep, indulging in wine at lunch at outdoor trattorias—enjoying our state of peace, togetherness, and relaxation. We buy fresh vegetables for our juice drink at the outdoor produce stand, Ortofrutta in Piazza di S.Pier Maggiore. This is an old green farm cart with red wooden wheels. An awning with strings of garlic hanging overhead protects the vegetables and fruit, hand-selected by Rosa, her brother Giuseppe, and his wife. They work six days a week, from eight in the morning until seven in the evening, regardless of the weather.

My best story of the week takes place on Sunday afternoon. We are having lunch at our favorite outdoor restaurant, Buca Poldo, with our Florentine friend Francesco, who is 48, handsome, and perpetually single. A much younger woman with an older man enters the terrace and they are seated across from us. I assume she is with her father and suggest she may be the perfect woman for Francesco. But the couple starts to hold hands and kiss. Then, he drops some food on his lap. The gorgeous young woman opens her purse, takes out a short can of *Bio Shout Viavà*, a dry cleaner in a can, and sprays it on the guys lap. She then takes what looks like a shoe brush out of her purse, kneels down in front of him and buffs the area. Are we really witnessing this public display of kinkiness? Thankfully they are not Americans. Otherwise, I'd have to apologize to someone.

On the Tuesday of our second week, we decide to hire David, our friend of 13 years, to take us out to the Chianti hills to scout vistas for what will be Maestro's Florentine painting projects this year. It is a glorious day as we meet up and plot our trip.

It takes longer than usual to get out of Florence because the World Cycling Championship is taking place this week in and around the city. Many of the streets have been blocked off and the rest are one way. The road races start in Montecatini Terme and Lucca before heading to Florence for a twisting 16.6 km finishing circuit that includes a 4.6 km climb to Fiesole. The elite men's race is over 279 km, and includes several other climbs and a loop through the center of Renaissance Florence, passing right in front of our building, before 10 laps of the finishing circuit. Elite women will race for 134.7 km and cover five laps of the finishing circuit. Despite Tuscany being one of the historic strongholds of Italian cycling, the central Italian region has never hosted the world championships.

Eventually, with David's expertise, we arrive at our first stop. *Poggio Alloro* is a breathtakingly beautiful estate with an ancient, perfectly restored farmhouse, cattle, and acres of olive groves and grape vines. Bill loves the spectacular vistas of the town of San Gimignano in the background and takes many photos. David never ceases to amaze us by finding new places, charming vineyards, and *fattorias* where they produce their own wine and olive oil.

David, of Irish decent, grew up in London. While traveling around the United States, the tall, red-haired charmer met an attractive Florentine woman. They got married, moved to her family home outside of Florence, and had two children. David speaks Italian with an accent of English working-class London. When he says "Chianti," it comes out, "Ki-ant-i."

It is too early for wine tasting and lunch, so we purchase some extra virgin organic olive oil, along with a few bottles of white wine, and head off to the Medieval Tuscan town of San Gimignano, 56 km south of Florence. David leaves us at the gate and Bill and I agree to meet him in several hours.

The historic center of San Gimignano contains a series of masterpieces of 14th- and 15th-century Italian art in their original architectural settings, including, in the cathedral, the fresco of the *Last Judgment, Heaven and Hell* by Taddeo di Bartolo (1393), the *Martyrdom of S. Sebastian* by Benozzo Gozzoli, and above all the magnificent frescoes by Domenico Ghirlandaio, like the cycle of Santa Fina and the Annunciation in the St John Baptistry. Other works of the same outstanding beauty include the huge frescoes by Benozzo Gozzoli depicting Saint Sebastian and Saint Augustine.

We stroll around the narrow, historic redbrick pavement with irregular triangular patterns to Palazzo Comunale on the southern side of Piazza del Duomo. Inside is the famous room, the Sala di Dante, which is decorated with important collections of courtly frescoes, and the Picture Gallery with its works dating back to the 13th through 17th centuries.

We decide on dell'Olmo in the Piazza della Cisterna for lunch-- not far from the wellhead, which dates back to 1237. We sit outside and absorb the timeless, magical atmosphere that prevails, taking in the ancient buildings and towers that alternate in perfect harmony all around the square.

We have been to Siena many times, but San Gimignano is even dearer to us—smaller and quainter with delightful shops selling works of art, jewelry, handmade embroidery and pottery. Despite the fact that theirs is a tourist business, meaning they may never see the customer again, the food is delicious; homemade pasta with wild boar sauce for my husband; ribollita, a typical Tuscan vegetable soup with bread, and a grilled cheese and ham "toast" for me. We wash the food down with a pitcher of the straw-yellow color local wine, Vernaccia di San Gimignano.

We spot a sign across the piazza boasting "the best gelato in the world" and listing the gelateria's winning years at the gelato festival. We know there really is such a festival with contenders from all over the country. "That's a no brainer," my husband says. So we treat ourselves to a cup of half dark chocolate and half pistachio and decide that it truly is great. Gelateria Dondoli does not disappoint. As we leave, directly across the courtyard we see yet another gelateria boasting of "the best gelato in the world." Can there be two "best in the world?" Not to mention our beloved Vivoli.

We return to Florence and find that UCI world road race championship in Tuscany has created a grand slam nightmare traffic situation. Helicopters loom overhead. The streets are blocked off with barricades and banners, and the race is going by in front of our building. Speeding down the empty street is a police motorcycle, red lights blinking, sirens blaring. This signifies another biker is coming. The crowds hover closer to the sidewalk barrier. Usually, a single biker flies by in seemingly perfect position. Onlookers cheer him with shouts of, *"Andole!"* (Spanish), *"Andiamo!"* (Italian) and various other languages. Immediately following the bike is a car with bike rack on top carrying an extra bike or bikes, and behind this car is a motorcycle with two men—the one behind is wearing a shirt with the word "doctor" on the back in large block letters. It's all very exciting and all happens at the speed of lightening.

The good news is that our apartment has an interior elevator. The bad news is that Bill got trapped inside and couldn't get out. There is a phone inside the elevator—for just such occasions—which connects to either one of the extensions in the apartment or to an outside line. I am sitting at the computer writing when the phone rings and it's Bill. "Where are you?" "I'm in the living room, where are you? I thought I heard you come down." "I'm trapped in the elevator and can't get out," he says.

He keeps his finger on the button and rides the hydraulic lift down to the laundry room and is able to get the downstairs door open and escape. The door on the main floor is broken. Now, the question is, how long will it take the Italian "technician" to get here and fix it? We don't want to be too pushy because we don't want the owner to think it is too much trouble to deal with us and decide to sell.

The following day Bill decides to try and fix the elevator himself and gets trapped once more. If you ever watched the Tim Allen show, where he portrays the ultimate un-handyman—well, that might as well be my husband. He just does not have the necessary skills to fix anything. He phones the building manager, who sends over Enrique, the handyman, who gets him out but is unable to fix the elevator. Thanks to the bicycle races in the city center, the technician is not working on any elevators in the city today. He will come at 9 a.m. Monday morning. So we go down a flight of stairs and enter from that floor, and then up an outside spiral staircase to the studio where Bill starts working on his large canvas. Today is Friday and we will wait till Monday—we have no choice!

The temperature has been about perfect, with high 70s by day and 60s in the evening. At the end of the day, we walk to Natalino, our neighborhood wine bar on Borgo degli Albizi. There are benches in front where people sit and watch the world go by. We find our friend and recent widower one evening. He tells us sitting on the bench and having a *vino*, scrutinizing the scene, is better than YouTube. The talk turns inevitably to climate conditions. "Sunday, it will rain," Massimo says. His friend concurs. *"Piove."*

———

We are going to London to visit our friend Brian Johnson for his birthday. We walk to the Florence Santa Maria Novella Train Station and buy our tickets so we can take the train to Pisa for our flight to London. On the way home we try an Argentinian restaurant, Pub 7 Secoli on Via Ghibellina, for an appetizer before heading, in the now pouring rain, into the alley to L'Antico Noè, a colorful Tuscan restaurant, which occupies the premises of an old butcher's shop under the old Arco di San Pierino. It's in our neighborhood and we have come to know the owner, Massimo Torelli, quite well.

Each day, Massimo rides his bicycle to the daily market of Sant'Ambrogio. He arrives back with baskets full of artichokes, zucchini flowers, porcini mushrooms, and whatever else is seasonal and fresh. He writes the menu of the day on brown paper and posts it on the window. This evening, he is excited to show us a fresh truffle that is under a glass cover. He smiles as he uncovers the rare fungus, so we can savor the delicate aroma. *"Maestro,"* he says delivering a big hug. He will shave truffle on the salad, make pasta with truffles, and even fry eggs with truffles. He brings me a plate of *uove con tartufo* and serves Bill the truffle-showered pasta. A pricey repast, but well worth the cost.

Bill is deeply involved with his new 6x10-foot soon-to-be masterpiece, *Vista of San Gimignano.* This will be the fourth massive painting he will be doing in the downstairs studio, and it will take about three months to complete this spectacular vista, with the city far off in the distance with its towers, which are famous throughout Italy. On the upper left side of the canvas is a small house and some terraced land and trees. He also does a small (24x30-inch) version of this image.

The elevator "technicians" arrive on time on Monday, along with the handyman. The prediction is once again for rain, so we will work around the weather. By 11, the elevator is fixed and I am thrilled to be able to ride it down to the laundry room and not bother Bill, who is painting upstairs. I pack the machine with all our dark colored clothes, Bill's assortment of black T- shirts, underwear, blue jeans, etc. and lock it up. The detergent enters through a pull-out drawer on the top. I add the usual detergent, emptying the box, but it's not enough. I spot a quart-size white bottle that says something about laundering directions in Italian but I do not pay attention to the word *candeggiare*. So I think I will add some of the liquid into the drawer. The machine accepts it and continues the inflow of water. Suddenly I am overpowered by the aroma of bleach. I have now just added a cup of bleach to a full load of our dark-colored laundry. Panic!

I spin the cycle manually and pull out the knob to stop it and try to get the water emptied before all the clothes have been touched. There is a three-minute delay before the door will open (safety precaution) and by the time I get the door open I am hoping I can salvage at least the new blue jeans that Bill has recently become addicted to. The door finally opens; I pull all the clothes out and put them in the sink, running cold water on them to rinse out any bleach before it can do its damage.

The front-loading washing machine takes just under two hours on the "short cycle." I peer through the glass door in an attempt to spot early damages. Finally the cycle is complete and I wait the three *long* minutes for the door to unlatch. I remove each item gingerly, with particular concentration on my husband's jeans; so far, so good. Bravo! No mutilations other than a few small bleach circles on one pair of my underwear. I hang the clothes on the rack to dry. The marriage is saved again—and life goes on.

A day later, the laundry has dried—always a long process, particularly in the rain and humid weather. Bill's black underwear and black T-shirts are now shaded with subdued orange circles which were not possible to see when wet. The Maestro will have to go tie-dye for at least a while.

The biweekly *Florentine*, the largest English language news magazine in Tuscany, has requested an interview with the Maestro. They will profile him as the expat feature of the week in an upcoming edition.

A young, attractive, recent college graduate from Saint Andrews, University of Scotland, Catriona Miller, newly employed by the paper, arrives half an hour late. This is her first assignment. She has done her homework and has checked out Bill's website. She knows what direction she would like her story to take and has questions in hand. Her father, an art history professor, is familiar with Bill's work, so she is enthusiastic about her interview. After a brief writer-to-writer chat, I leave them to the task. She spends several hours, takes many photos of Bill, and his recent works and discusses the paintings in progress for her article.

The article comes out on Thursday, November 7, featuring my darling husband, the expatriate painter living in Florence. The headline is in large bold letters: "William Kelley, Painting the Soul of Tuscany." There is a two-page spread with photos of his paintings. It starts out:

A few streets over from Michelangelo's former home, William Kelley and his wife, Susan, have settled in a beautiful flat with panoramic views of Florence. Since 2004, the American-born artist has made Florence a permanent base, first renting a studio on the Ponte Vecchio. When the space proved too small for his work—the large oil-on-canvas landscapes for which he is best known—he frequently changed studios in Florence as well as spending time at his atelier in Sarasota, Florida.

"Wow," Bill says. "I never thought I'd see the day that I was mentioned in the same sentence as Michelangelo." Catriona has written a flattering story with beautifully displayed photos of several paintings, including his massive 7x15-foot *Tuscan Soul.* She continues;

> A big change occurred in 1999, when Kelley decided to study art in Florence. He completed two semesters at the Lorenzo de Medici Art Institute, focusing on conceptual painting and art history, and then spent a few months at a time in various Florentine studios before settling here for good in 2004.

I email the link from the article all over the U.S. and London to friends, relatives, and collectors of his artwork. He has now gone beyond "Maestrohood." We get a bunch of extra copies and deliver them to our friends and favorite local restaurants and to Rosa at the corner vegetable stand. *"Va bene,"* she says, duly impressed. *"Avanti, il tappeto rosso."* Next, the red carpet!

Return to Casali di Bibbiano

We first visited Casali di Bibbiano, an 18th-century country estate, a year ago while driving around the rolling hills of Tuscany on a perfect sunny autumn day and stopping over at local vineyards. We were so impressed with the beauty and peaceful atmosphere of Bibbiano, we knew we had to return for a longer stay. And now that he knew there was a Sarasota/Tuscan connection, Alberto had invited us back.

We took the two-hour train ride from our home in Florence, and Alberto picked us up at Buonconvento station. Driving in his black Audi, we wind our way down the long stately drive, lined on either side with soaring cypress trees. We are greeted at the gate by the charming guest-relations coordinator, Claudia Zeni. We check into our large airy room: "Il Girasole," the sunflower.

Lunch is served on the terrace overlooking the vine-clad hills and silvery-gray olive groves. The panoramic view is mesmerizing, and there is no sound. We are served a crisp white wine, Primo Bacio, with our meal of homemade pasta with fresh tomatoes and basil from the garden, and gnocchi in a pesto sauce. A platter of cured salami, prosciutto, olives, and cheese follows. Alberto joins us for a discussion of wines produced in Italy and why they are so good. The grapes must be picked at the exact time they are ready and sent to production. Weather dictates when this will take place. If there are too many rainy days or flooding, the harvest must wait. The regulation for low sulfites is very strict, he explains, and every plant is inspected. Thus we are able to drink more wine with no side effects. Alberto says that his guests are always commenting on how much wine they consume in Italy and how they never experience a headache. The lower sulfites are the reason.

We are introduced to Chef Massimiliano "Max" Izzo, who is preparing fresh handmade pasta for this evening's dinner. He is toasting walnuts for the sauce and yes, they are from the walnut trees on the property.

After lunch, Alberto is excited to find out that both he and Bill share a love of golf. It so happens that the all-new, quite spectacular golf club, Castiglione del Bosco, built by the Ferragamo family, borders his property, and he entices my husband to go and "hit a few balls." It does not take a lot of persuasion. I admonish them not to be gone too long, as I leave for a walk around the property, camera in hand.

Claudia takes me through the wine-making procedure and into the wine cellars. I notice buckets of freshly picked large green olives; these are for eating, she explains, not for the oil. The olives for the oil are not ready for picking till mid- or late-November, depending on the vagaries of rain and sun—like the grapes.

Afterward, I return to the kitchen to talk to the chef. He graciously shares some of his "secret" recipes. You will not gain weight on the typical Tuscan diet. Nor will you find massive plates of meatballs and spaghetti. Instead, your taste buds will come alive with the flavors of Tuscany: the freshest fruits and vegetables, superb cheeses, meats fresh from the local butcher.

Food is always one of the great Italian passions and tonight we are in for a gastronomic feast. The fresh *tagliolini* is drying on the racks; sauce is simmering. The massive Chianina beefsteaks now marinating will become the famous *Bistecca alla Fiorentina*.

Alberto gives me his tip for a marinade: olive oil, a pinch of salt and pepper, and some fresh rosemary. Once the steak has been seared over hot coals and is sliced rare, the juice of the meat mixes with the marinade to form an exquisite flavor. The chef gathers the five fingers of his right hand to his lips and air kisses them while simultaneously tossing the kiss to the universe.

Chef Izzo's gourmet four-course dinner with unlimited wines from the Casali di Bibbiano's winery is served nightly on the terrace or in the restaurant, and vegetarians can be accommodated, despite the emphasis on beefsteak.

October ends the season, so the guest numbers are dwindling and we are invited to sit at the family table for dinner. Two of Alberto's four children, Andrea and Gabriella, have stayed to work at the property and will join us, in addition to Alberto and Massimilliano. Another of his sons, Marco, works at Saluté in Sarasota, along with Andrea.

I asked Alberto where he would rather be, here or Sarasota. "Both places give you a lot of energy. I like to be both places." We agree.

We order some cases of the wine to be shipped to Florence, where we can have a wine tasting with friends, and we are sad to leave our new "family." We know we will return and stay even longer the next time.

Max gives me his recipe for Tagliolini with toasted walnuts. It's very loose, no quantities; he must think I'm his equal as a chef.

Tagliolini (light and delicate)

Toast walnuts in oven or fry pan.

In pan, sauté 1 stick unsalted butter, splash of olive oil, chopped onion, and chopped pancetta. (Can use bacon or salami.)

Add splash of white wine, stir, and simmer ten minutes.

Tear a couple of basil leaves and toss in (he tossed them, seriously).

Cook pasta in boiling water for 2 minutes.

Add pasta to sauce and sprinkle with parmesan.

(Sometimes, the chef grates lemon rind on top.)

Although we were there just a few days, Bill does numerous paintings from this trip, most of which I love so much that I don't want to part with them. Later, I have a story accepted by *Sarasota Magazine* called "The Tuscany-Sarasota Connection."

Our new fabulous find this year for our morning cappuccino is Cantinetta dei Verrazzano (an extra z in the spelling) on via Dei Tavolini 18—central but off the beaten track. It has a superb bakery, where they produce their own focaccia-- a flat, oven-baked Italian bread which is filled with a variety of all the best and freshest seasonal ingredients like peas and prosciutto and cheese. This is a perfect spot for a light lunch or a snack. We also like to go on a rainy November afternoon and soak up the atmosphere, huddling over a platter of paper-thin prosciutto and cheeses with honey, or baked cheese crostini with 10-year-old balsamic vinegar. Only recently did we find that they serve espresso and cappuccino; it is about the best around and at 1.20 euros, among the cheapest. For 1 euro, you can also pick up a gorgeous chocolate filled croissant – and we do. Sometimes, Bill orders a fresh squeezed *spremuta di melograno* (pomegranate juice). We have now incorporated it into our morning walk, the croissant and the pedometer. I can see how many calories I've burned, although they are surely offset by the croissants.

Verrazzano also operates a vineyard in Greve in Chianti, one hour outside of Florence. The property has been famous for many years as a producer of high quality Chianti Classico wines. Several years ago we went on a tour. Gino Rosi, our guide and host, took us through the Verrazzano castle, gardens, and historic cellar. He told us the Verrazzano name comes from a mix of two Latin words meaning "land of the wild boars." The bridge, famous in New York, is named for Florentine explorer Giovanni da Verrazano, who became the first European to enter New York Harbor and the Hudson River. Gino himself, a colorful character, bonded with Bill because he had lived in Amherst near the University of Massachusetts, where Bill attended college.

Bill went for his first-of-the-year Italian haircut at my encouragement. His hair, blondish white--no make that whitish blonde--was way too long and flipping up; he was starting to take on the appearance of a homeless artist instead of a successful one. Off to Antonio of Antonio E Marcello at Piazza Dè Salterelli for an 11 a.m. appointment.

At noon, he arrived back, unrecognizable—short brown hair, brown eyebrows, and a huge smile. He claims to have fallen asleep in the chair and not known what happened. For some bizarre reason, the barbers in Florence put a rinse or dye on men's hair as a matter of course and I guess the eyebrows as well. He assures me that it will wash out. In fact, it did.

La Dolce Vita, Florentine Style

This year's style phenomenon is a new look for men—skinny pants and bare ankles. Italy definitely influences the way the rest of the world dresses. Here among the city's cobblestone streets, looking oh so carefree, yet very studied, are the young Italian men, wearing a combination of colorful patterns and textures, accessorized with silk scarves or pocket squares and perhaps even a lapel pin

Even my Bill dresses in a different manner in Italy. I notice that here he pays more attention to what goes on his newly svelte (since he gave up bread) body. He layers a long sleeve shirt over a golf shirt with a colored T-shirt underneath. He wears a colorful scarf, doubling it and looping it around his neck. I like the transformation of a guy who used to be happy in a baggy shirt.

November first, All Saints Day is a major Catholic holiday in Florence, but the spa is open and I am here for a noon pedicure. *Bless me father for I have sinned, it's been 7 weeks since my last pedicure.*

If you're looking for a decent manicure or pedicure in Florence, you're in for a big disappointment.

"They just don't get nails here," my Florentine friend says. "That's the bottom line."

I've asked every woman I know about nail salons, and have followed several leads. Last year I arrived at Salon Mario for a scheduled appointment. The woman at the reception desk seemed disappointed that I was not there for a haircut, which I undoubtedly needed.

I look forward to my monthly pedicure in the States. It's a treat to sink into the oversized massaging chair, rest my head, and soak my weary feet in the warm gurgling water. Each foot is removed lovingly, manicured, and placed back in the water while the other is being worked on until they are both buffed and massaged and ready for my happy toes to be painted and back on the road.

The version here is quite different. The esthetician sits in a folding metal chair and I sit on an identical one facing her. She puts a bucket on the floor and instructs me to stick one foot in. She has the tools of the trade on her lap. *"Salve,"* she says. This is a little more formal than *"Ciao"* and a little less than *"Buongiorno."* I am focused on the metal tools and wonder if they have been properly sanitized.

We converse in Italian. About a minute later, I am instructed to take my foot from the pail of water and put it on her lap. At this time, the other foot goes into the bucket. In this uncomfortable position, she files, snips, pushes the cuticles back, and paints my toenails. All is completed in one fell swoop. Only then does the other foot comes out of the bucket and the identical procedure follows. The process is complete in less than half an hour and it is not at all relaxing.

This year, I keep looking for a better place, so I Google the Four Seasons Hotel thinking they must have sterilized equipment and offer a more luxurious treatment. The basic pedicure takes 50 minutes at a cost of 90 euro, roughly $116 at today's exchange rate. I can't bring myself to spend that. The "luxury pedicure" goes for 120 euro ($155 at today's rate.) I decide to keep looking.

I take a friend's advice and schedule a time with Mina, her new *find* at Gabrio Staff Olimpo on Via de'Tornabuoni, a full-service spa. She has assured me that they have an actual pedicure chair, or at least a reasonable facsimile. After pressing her, she admits it is marginally better than the folding metal chair and plastic bucket of water at Mario's, but it's an elevated bench with an actual foot-soaking tub.

I arrive at the attractive spa, with its polite and friendly staff. Mina, mid-20s and curvaceous with a sensuous painted mouth, is yet another gorgeous Florentine woman. Her cascading, dark, wavy hair with henna highlights is complemented by a low-cut black sweater, black leggings, and white wedge sneakers with black laces. She sits on her stool in front of me and snaps on black latex gloves, now taking on the appearance of a dominatrix.

She gets to work removing the equipment from sealed packages so I am assured that they must be sterilized. I've brought my own polish and I've worn sandals so I won't smudge my toes on the walk home. Mina speaks no English but we get by nicely.

I sit and peruse the list of other spa services available: an oxygen facial where they apparently shoot oxygen into your pores (non-invasive) for 130-230 euro is a temptation, but that's roughly half the cost of the Furla bag I have my eye on. I'll pass. The cost is a modest 40 euro for the pedicure, but it is over in 32 minutes and is not what I would call luxurious. Mina leans over and blows her breath on my toes to speed up drying before applying the top coat. *And we are done here!* She leaves.

Oops, not so fast. I sit alone watching my toes dry. Five minutes seem an hour. I attempt to slide my feet, ever so gingerly into my sandals and in doing so, smudge the big toe of my left foot. Now I must venture out and find Mina and beg her to fix it with my flip flops in place. She does; brilliant. I leave in a hurry before further damage occurs and I increase my tip.

I spend a fortune on Kérastase products—shampoo, conditioner and Cristal Sculpt—and hide them from my husband. But the water here is harsh with chemicals and my highlighted hair immediately shows the signs of stress. I seem to lose hair often, and I know it's more than the expected 100 strands a day—although I've not counted.

You can get a good haircut here, but you're best to look elsewhere for color. Red looks like a Crayola crayon and the blonde highlights like tiger stripes. I won't try a cut here—too traumatic.

I do have friends who reach beyond the basic hand, foot, and hair concerns. There is a Greek doctor who runs an esthetic medical clinic called *Skin* on Borgo San Jacopo. He does all kind of procedures like Botox and fillers; I have a buddy who goes to have her skin "ironed." Not exactly sure what that means, but she always looks great.

Sunday: The Country Lunch

One of the oldest Italian traditions is the Sunday family lunch. Several generations gather for a midday meal that goes on for hours. We always look forward to our annual trip to Ristorante Mario alla Querciola di Moscardi, in the Querciola Caldine section of Fiesole, for "the steak" with Corso and his wife, Bei, who now eats meat after moving here from China. They are part of our extended Florentine family. Although the trattoria is billed as a mere "10 minutes from Firenze," it's really more like 25 minutes before we arrive at the large nondescript concrete building with *"Ristorante Mario"* printed across the front in large letters. The parking area is packed, but Corso manages to maneuver and invent a new space for his car, and we are ushered into our 1:30 reservation in the large room with a window opening into the busy kitchen. This is a rustic, family atmosphere that extends over four rooms. Today being, Sunday, and the end of a holiday weekend means the restaurant is filled with many local families. We have never seen any tourists here and this is our fourth year. Featuring classic, typical Tuscan cuisine, Mario is famous for its *bistecca alla Fiorentina*. The rest of the menu consists of about eight possibilities of vegetables, large enough for sharing and each costing just 3 euro. We order an antipasto of *insalata di rucola zucchini e pinole al balsamico*. We all agree that no one wants pasta. Le Volte wine, a Bill favorite, is a mere 19 euros per bottle; we order several. All of this arrives with bread and the newly pressed, unfiltered olive oil.

The piece de resistance arrives and is placed at center table: a massive, charcoal-grilled T-bone. The chef has sliced it while leaving it intact, making it easy to serve. I help myself to a few slices of the tenderloin and everyone dives in. The olive oil is poured generously over the white beans and roasted red peppers. There are homemade French fries, spinach and more. We sit for hours, sipping wine and enjoying the food despite a noisy family behind us with two very badly behaved and loud children. Mid-meal, Corso turns and addresses the children directly; I'm thinking this is a breach of protocol, but he is Florentine so he should know the rules. He tells them, "Don't you think you should relax and take a nap? Please, we are trying to eat!" The kids quiet down for about five minutes before resuming their raucous running around the restaurant, bumping into tables and pushing each other. When the family gets up to leave, the mother rebukes Corso, telling him that they are children after all. Corso's response is to order another bottle of wine. For dessert, a dark, dense chocolate cake baked with pear arrives and we taste it with the red wine; orgasmic. We are the last to leave at 4 p.m. And there is no need for dinner tonight.

Giorno del Ringraziamento

We both have been working constantly, and November is coming to a close. We think we've earned a day off and it is a brilliantly sunny Saturday morning as we head to Perini, now our favorite traditional food market in Mercato Centrale, to buy some cheese and to deliver a copy of the *Florentine* featuring Bill's article. *"Ciao, Maestro,"* Andrea says the moment he spots us. He immediately starts slicing prosciutto—paper thin—on the massive machine, piling it on slices of just-baked Tuscan bread along with slabs of cheese. He stands behind the raised glass counter displaying an assortment of cheeses and charcuterie, as well as gourmet specialties with balsamic vinegar, extra-virgin olive oil, and Alba truffles. He hands us a plastic cup of red wine. *"No grazie, è troppo presto."* It's too early. *"Oh- Dio-mio!* Oh my God," he says making a face and insisting we accept the *vino*; there is no turning it down.

Once Bill is out on a day like this, he refuses to go home. Every tiny café and trattoria seem to beckon him, "Come in, Maestro, have a little wine!" We leave the market and walk to Piazza della Repubblica for our annual terrace lunch at the Savoy hotel;

the absolute best people-watching place in the city. Bill orders a chicken club sandwich and I have the carrot soup with ginger. No one ever rushes us as we stay for hours watching the passersby

This is the weekend where the farmers come in with their new harvest olive oil and present their fresh production at individual tasting stalls in Piazza della Repubblica. There is a winter chill in the air and the vendors, bundled up, stand behind the tables offering samples of small squares of crunchy Tuscan bread to be dipped in the fresh, unfiltered, green virgin olive oil. I walk from booth to booth, sampling the wares, and buy several bottles of organic oil from Le Colline di Vinci, a 17th-century farmhouse overlooking the hills of Vinci. From another vendor I buy packets of *peperoncino,* a hot pepper to toss into a variety of sauces—all organic. I prefer the spicier green oil and tend to purchase from the same vendors each year. Another favorite is San Leo. Once you've tasted the fresh-made extra virgin olive oil of Tuscany, you are spoiled forever and you will want to take it home with you.

Herein lies the problem. A liter bottle of the new oil may cost 15 euro, but it costs 20 euro a bottle to ship it to the states. Or you can pack it in the suitcase you are traveling with and risk being charged overweight baggage or spillage, or both. Either way, it's worth it. The oil is sold in cans as well as bottles, but Florentines will tell you that it tastes better from the bottle. Here I also buy some fresh made honey and cheese.

Now it is almost Thanksgiving and it is finally cold—in the 30s to 40s and windy; we are bundled up. My oldest and best friend in the States seems to always find something she has read about that she wants me to buy here and bring back. Generally, the information is incorrect and I am on a last minute wild goose chase around the city, like the time she wanted me to buy her a Ferragamo scarf at the Uffizi gallery for $20, and when I got there it was $350. This year is no exception. She has the list of what to buy in Florence from the latest edition of *Travel + Leisure.* If it's not too much trouble, could I go to San Lorenzo market and find the place that embroiders names on stuff while you wait? She would love an apron monogrammed with her name in Italian, *"Giovanna,"* and would it be too much to ask for one for her granddaughter (Ava) as well? "Wouldn't that be so much fun to wear them together on Christmas?" she asks.

I think I have seen a store that does this, right on Via de' Calzaiuoli, but I trek past the Duomo and turn left, only to find yet another gelato store has opened in its place. I come home and Google "embroidered aprons, Florence," and happily I find one listed with an address in Piazza San Lorenzo, 35 red. At five o'clock, I head out to the market, but I am unable to find it and it is cold.

I start to ask vendors and am directed to a wagon near the Mercato Centrale—and sure enough there is a woman selling embroidered goods: aprons and potholders and such, and she does it by machine, while I wait. It's not the place I was looking for but they have what I am looking for. I opt for the simple red with white lettering. On Ava's they write her name on the bib and on the bottom, *Oggi, Cucino io,* "I'm cooking today." This is what friends are for and I really am happy to provide this service to my dearest and very best friend.

Today is *Giorno del Ringraziamento,* Thanksgiving, and this year we have opted for a trip to Venice. Bill has completed this year's painting production and we are ready for a celebration. We will be taking the train to Santa Lucia railway station and then the *vaporetto* (water bus) to St. Marco. Then we will walk to The Europa and Regina Hotel, where we will spend a night. Sunday we will cook the turkey and celebrate with Mary and Mario.

It's cold as we board the morning train, but it's not raining. We have been to Venice many times since our first visit 16 years ago. Venice is not so much fun when it's flooded, and you have to walk on planks. The pleasant train ride takes just over two hours. There is nothing quite as spectacular as exiting the S. Lucia railway station and finding yourself standing in front of the Grand Canal. No cars, no bikes; just water and boats. We walk to the Vaporetto station and take the number 2 waterbus to the San Marco Vallaresso stop, which takes about 45 minutes. From here it is an easy walk to the hotel. We check into the beautiful canal-front hotel and I say it is Thanksgiving (true) and our anniversary (not true) and we are immediately upgraded to a lagoon-view room.

It is a brilliant, sunny day with blue skies, and we bundle up against the cold and head to St. Marks for some tea and a panini. We walk and walk and explore, up and down stairs and over bridges and through alleys on our way to the Peggy Guggenheim Collection, a modern art museum on the Grand Canal, an attraction we never miss.

Toward evening, we walk to Harry's Bar for the mandatory *bellini*—Prosecco and fresh peach juice for 16.50 euros each. I have only one.

Venice is even more magical than usual, fully decked with the Christmas decorations and lights. We decide it is too cold for a gondola ride; maybe tomorrow. We have made a reservation for dinner at Da Forno, and we head to the hotel's Tiepolo bar for an *aperitivo*.

We meet Aldo, the bartender, and in conversation, we find out he has known our friend Mario for over 30 years and that they used to work together.

He brings two complimentary drinks and offers us an alternative dining option—al Paradiso Ristorante in San Polo, which he describes as excellent and not touristy. We decide to give it a shot, and he calls and makes us a reservation. After a long walk, we find the place to be cozy and delightful with excellent food.

The next day, on the way to the train around 3 p.m., we stop for a late lunch at Osteria La Patatina. I order fried shrimp and zucchini—not very good; Bill has warned against shellfish. He has pasta. But it's Venice, which is known for *its fish dishes*. We take the train back to Florence and go for a neighborhood dinner of tagliolini with duck sauce—at least that is what I had. At one in the morning I awake with the worst case of food poisoning, which lasts double-barrel till 7 a.m., non-stop. Another good feature about this apartment is the bidet. I was able sit on the toilet sideways and heave into the bidet simultaneously. I know now that I could never be bulimic.

Did the food poisoning come from the shrimp in Venice or the duck sauce in Florence? Upon Googling food poisoning on three sites, I find that shellfish is listed as the number one culprit.

I awake Saturday; have I really been sick? It all seems surreal. It was during the night, so I didn't miss any days. I drink a 1.5-liter bottle of water and eat nothing.

Bill and I walk as planned to the Macelleria Mononi to pick up the organic turkey. It's not a holiday in Florence, so all stores and markets are open. A few feathers are apparent as Sandro, cradling the bird, displays him proudly, as if he were showing off his newborn son. Weighing in at 7.12 kilo—about 15 ½ pounds. We lower the carefully wrapped treasure into the shopping trolley and we are off to the vegetable stand to buy apples and walnuts for stuffing and potatoes and green beans and, yes the squash-- but I buy spaghetti squash by mistake. Who cares, we'll put it on the table for color—at least it's orange. We wheel this all back home in our cart.

Once home, Bill rinses out the bird with 15-year-old Dalwhinnie Single Malt scotch whiskey—using almost ¾ of the bottle. With love, he places it in the pan and bastes it with one stick of butter and a bottle of white wine every hour for the next five hours. The result is not only the moistest and most delicate and tender turkey, but also the best tasting gravy you can imagine. Last year a friend tasted my gravy and asked, "Who made the soup? Mary and the always-dapper Mario bring homemade vegetable soup and chocolate cake for dessert.

The week following the holiday is usually one of the busiest of the year for us. Suddenly it's December and shipping day. David picks us up on schedule at 11am and we load up the van with the now wrapped and rolled 6-foot-tall canvas, along with nine other paintings, which are still on their stretchers. We have opted to ship the olive oil this year in an effort to avoid weight overages on our luggage leaving Pisa, as well as one very heavy suitcase loaded with books and CDs and shoes. Last year one suitcase was 3 kilos overweight and I was on my hands and knees at Pisa airport searching for books and any other heavy item to remove. Bill is sad to see his work of three months leaving for the states but is happy with his production.

———

Bill is taking David for a thank you lunch at San Domenico Ristorante near Fiesole. I must rush home and meet the new handyman who will try to fish for the seat cushion that blew off our terrace and landed on the tile roof below us. The hook on the rope is not hooking its target; it keeps dislodging roof tiles and cable wires. He leaves and returns with poles that he tapes together. In 15 minutes he manages to flip the cushion on to the deck below.

I come home and make the turkey soup. Once cleaned up, with the turkey carcass in a trash bag, I venture out—cash in hand—to Furla, in pursuit of the purple bag I want, even though Bill strongly suggests it is shallow to buy another purse. It is sold out! It is disappointing because I wanted it for my board lunch for SPARCC, my organization against domestic violence. I am meeting Bill at the Savoy for our first inside-the-hotel cocktail of the year. Then we will come home for the soup.

We are off today for our annual leave-taking, visiting museums, Christmas shopping, and who knows what else? Once the paintings are shipped, Maestro has to say goodbye to just about everyone in Firenze. I never know where we will end up.

We walk to Rivoire for a cappuccino and then to the Uffizi, the oldest gallery in modern Europe. The main purpose of our visit is to see the three new Rembrandt paintings on display. It's best to come here with a definite plan, otherwise you will get lost in hours of over stimulation. We climb the many stairs and walk down the long hallway to the Botticelli room, my personal favorite. We never tire of viewing his greatest works, *The Birth of Venus* and *La Primavera*. We continue to Rembrandt. Bill dons his reading glasses and looks closely at the great portraits carefully studying the brush strokes and the master's use of color. He sums up his reaction, and mine, with one word, "Great," he says.

Now on to the Strossi Palace for a Russian Avant-Garde show: Siberia and the Orient featuring works of Kandinsky and Malevič, among others. For lunch, we return to Osteria Nuvoli on Piazza dell'Olio near the Duomo. We were here only once, in 2001, with

Bill's teachers, Rose and Claire, while he was a student at *Scuola Lorenzo de'Medici*.

For some reason we have not gone back, but today seems the perfect time. It is tiny and homey in the downstairs *cantine*. The food is delicious and very inexpensive. No tourists are here. We are seated on long backless benches at community tables. The owner's wife tells Bill he must have the *polpette con piselli*—meatballs with peas. No arm twisting is necessary. I have delicate cheese ravoli with ragu sauce and it is perfect.

Our last Friday in Florence this year and for lunch we decide to check out the new place owned by the butcher originally from Greve, in Chianti, where he is famous for being Sting's butcher. He has opened a little spot practically across the courtyard from Noè.

There is a place to order your food and a room with a large community table where you can eat. We order a board of prosciutto and cheese on Tuscan bread and a tomato soup. We pay in advance and they hand me a paper cup with the soup and tell me I can microwave it in the back room. Hmmm. Bill has ordered us a glass of wine but they give him a prepaid card which, when put in the Enomatic wine serving system slot, delivers whatever amount of wine you have paid for. This is an interesting experience but Luca at Noè, whom Bill refers to as "Marty

Muscle," makes the best toasted panini for 4 euro, and he doesn't measure out the wine. It will remain our lunch place of choice. It's hard to beat.

The exit plan continues as Bill needs to say goodbye to every person—in person—at every restaurant. The Christmas shopping begins and we are happy to be here on December 8, the feast of the Immaculata, when all the lights are turned on. Our Christmas shopping always includes a trip to Philip, directly across from the famous Bronze Boar at Mercato Nuovo on Via Porta Rossa and Via Por Santa Maria. Philip is a former professional soccer star from Romania, who because of a knee injury changed careers. He now stands all day selling T-shirts, sweatshirts, hats, soccer shirts, and aprons from his cart. Can all that standing be good for his knee, I wonder?

Sunday will be our final dinner with the entire family at Buca Poldo. Both Donatello and Luciano and their mother, along with their wives and combined four children; both sons named Francesco. When their father was terminally ill in Calabria, he called his sons to his deathbed with an emotional request. He asked that if either of his sons had a son, they would promise to name the boy after him, Francesco.

Donatello and his wife Nora were the first to have a son and named him Francesco. Luciano and his wife Alisa had two daughters before she gave birth to their son, whom they also named Francesco. We hug and play with the children, ages five, four, two and one. Bill draws pictures of Mickey Mouse and Santa Claus.

The next day, we are on our way to Pisa and back to the States for the holidays.

—⁂—

When we return in the fall of 2014, we realize that over the course of the past 15 years, we have been spending from three to eight months a year living and working in Florence. We have had numerous house guests and visitors, ranging from a rock star (AC/DC's Brian Johnson) to a contemplative nun (art historian Sister Wendy Beckett) tell us we are "living the dream," and that I should be writing about it. I decide that now is the time.

My first task in returning is to meet Lisa at her home to review the recipes she gave me so many years ago. I tell her I am writing a book about living in Florence and want to add her recipes. She has insisted we try them out again, so that I can understand the steps perfectly. Once again, she has bought all the ingredients and has carefully laid out them out.

"Come on, let's have a little sip of wine to celebrate," she says in her signature voice. I tell her that Meryl Streep will play her in the movie; this delights her and she laughs heartily. At age 78, she is doing well and her eyesight is a little better after years of treatment. Marcello passed away while we were in Florida. "I have no one to fight with anymore," she says. "He was the love of my life; we were married for 30 years—one thing or another."

Bill's first order is to decide *what* he will paint this fall. To determine this, he will need to go to the country for inspiration. Belfast-born, Freddy Matson, our dear friend in Sarasota, is a sommelier and has set up a wine tasting for us at Caparzo, a top-producing vineyard and estate covering over 210 acres in Montalcino, where we are welcomed like royalty. Following a two hour tour of the pristine winery, we swirl and sip the Brunello Di Montalcino overlooking the gorgeous vineyards.

Freddy has also graciously set us up overnight at Borgo Scopeto Relais, part of the Caparzo group. This is a typical Tuscan estate turned exclusive hotel close to the city of Siena. After a great and fun two days of walking and exploring in this unforgettable pristine countryside, Bill says he has years of paintings in his head for the next ten years. "This will be the year of the grapes," he pronounces. We call our friend David to pick us up and take us home to Florence. Maestro is now ready to begin this year's production.

The first painting is a 5x6-foot scene, which he will work on in the downstairs studio. He makes a collage—composites from all the photos he has recently taken and had printed by Giovanni Fortunato Fotografo on Borgo degli Albizi. The grapes are highly exaggerated and take up half the painting, and are surrounded by some very strong yellows and greens from the vineyard. "I pushed the envelope on the background, making magenta fields with some green and blue trees," he says. There are some soft impressionistic hills in the deep background. Bill says that when he looks at it, he can almost see it as an abstract painting—but the more he looks, the more he focuses on the perspective and detail.

He starts three other canvasses, all with the same enormous grapes from different vantages. One is a 3x4-foot canvas with six bunches of grapes in the foreground, surrounded by hills and three olive trees. There is another painting in progress with two rows of grapes featuring the very strong reddish brown soil of the vineyard. Massimo Zecchi comes for a preview and calls the grapes *"la profonda anima del Chianti,"* the profound soul of Chianti. There is a more traditional landscape with the grapes, not as gigantic as the others and it has beautiful fields in the background. A non-grape painting includes one of seven cypress trees standing mightily in the foreground.

The Exit Plan

Our 25th wedding anniversary was in June. We decide we will celebrate throughout the year and we plan a trip to Rome and Vienna. Our non-stop flight is from Rome so we take the early train for a nostalgic return to our first city in Italy that we visited together in 1997. We retrace our steps—to the Pantheon and Pizazza Navona one of our favorite city squares to behold the Bernini statues, once again

I booked the InterContinental Wien through American Express and when asked if it is a special occasion, I told them yes; it is our anniversary. When we arrive, we are whisked away to the Club floor to be checked in and the general manager tells us we have been given a double upgrade. When we enter the room we see towels folded in the shape of swans, surrounded by red rose petals on the massive bed. Moments later, there is a knock on the door and a waiter enters wheeling in a cart with a bottle of champagne, two glasses, strawberries dipped in dark chocolate, and the world famous *Sachertorte*, a specific type of chocolate cake, invented by Austrian

Franz Sacher in 1832, of the famed Hotel Sacher, where it is served to this day, as well as throughout Vienna. "What's going on?" my husband asks, stunned. I tell him it's our anniversary celebration.

The city has magnificent museums and palaces and imposing architecture around the Ringstrasse, as well as the Spanish Riding School with its dancing Lipizzaner horses. My personal highlight is a detailed, guided tour of Schonburg Palace, with its fascinating history of Empress Elisabeth, the bride of Emperor Franz Joseph I. We also love Mozarthaus, where Mozart is said to have written *The Marriage of Figaro*. It is a thrill to see the most famous Gustav Klimt piece, *The Kiss*, at the Gallery Belvedere.

One thing we did not love was the massive traditional Viennese dishes of schnitzel, overlapping the plate, or the sausages and wurst, which are in no short supply. We find ourselves looking for an Italian restaurant. We settle on Do & Co, a stylish restaurant overlooking St. Stephen's Cathedral, which offers a lighter menu.

—⊷⊶—

Back in Florence, we are getting ready to wrap up our season; it does not get easier to leave. It's impossible to walk through the alley between Via del Oriuolo and Borgo D'Albizi without being stopped by

Massimo. Today we are walking home and he comes running after us, calling, "Maestro, Maestro." He wants Bill to taste a spoonful of veal in a tomato, basil and garlic sauce he is cooking, so he comes out with a small plate and a tumbler of red wine. "I'm never leaving." Bill says. "They love me in Italy."

Part of our exit plan includes inviting friends over to view Bill's art production of the period, before the paintings are shipped back to the states. This is a serious process, as our friends are very intense about painting. Art is something that has been ingrained in them from an early age. In fact, it is our friends Donatello and Nora who bring along their four-year-old, Francesco. He carries a book from preschool art class and he has a favorite painter that he shows Bill: "Vincent van Goat!" *"Mi piacciono i colori allegri."* He loves the happy colors of Bill's paintings. When they leave, little Francesco turns to Bill. *"Ciao,* Vincent van Goat!"

I've come up with a brilliant new easy idea for entertaining. Instead of cooking all day, I bring a large glass serving dish to Massimo at L'Antico Noè during his lunch time and ask him to fill it with prosciutto, mozzarella di bufala, and pomodori, which I will pick up in the evening. Massimo uses only the freshest and most genuine ingredients that he buys locally. We invite small groups to arrive at 6:30 p.m. when I offer nuts, olives, and wine. Bill takes them on the tour of both studios. At 7:30, we order pizza from Runner Pizza, our favorite take out place; it is delivered punctually in twenty minutes, hot and crispy. I serve this along with Massimo's delectable platter on our large round dining room table with the Duomo fully lit up and visible in the background.

The end of November draws near and Mary and I meet for a farewell lunch at Obikà, a mozzarella bar that is part of a world-wide chain. We see that it is now called Obicà with a "c." The menu now explains that "Obicà means, 'Here it is,'" something happening right before your eyes." We are happy to find they still serve the same great choices for lunch. It turns out that Obikà was never a Japanese name, but was a word in Neopolitan dialect all along.

This is the first year since we've been coming to Florence that there is concern for the new Tuscan olive oil production. Due to severe weather and fruit flies, the harvest has been greatly diminished. According to the news reports, the overall production will decrease by at least 40 percent and producers worry that due to the fruit fly infestations, the quality of the oil will be compromise.

Thanksgiving Eve and Bill is done. He has completed 11 new paintings and is ready to celebrate. On our way to Rivoire, we stop at a small men's shop on Via Del Corso that we pass daily. In the window is a wool cap Bill has been admiring.

The proprietor of the shop, dressed impeccably in blue jeans, brown loafers, a dress shirt, and a double-breasted jacket, sits at a wooden desk as we enter the shop named for the owner, Piero Puliti.

"*Buona sera*," Piero says, a dead ringer for Al Pacino. The brand is Stetson, but the hat is made in Donegal, Ireland. Bill tries on the biggest size, 62, and it fits. "*Stella de cinema*," he says, smiling. Movie star. Piero tells his wife to get the camera so he can be photographed with Maestro. He puts on the identical hat, stands on his toes with his arm around Bill, and smiles broadly.

This will be our final visit this year to the tiny Dante church in the center of Florence to view the *Presepio,* the nativity scene with the antique, almost life-size figurines. We sit on the uncomfortable ancient wooden benches, feeling grateful just for being here and listening to the haunting background music.

We have shipped the paintings to the states and we have a final week this season. Bill calls it "fun week," because neither of us work this week. One evening we walk over the Ponte Vecchio, beautifully decorated with Christmas lights, and go to Le volpi e l'uva, the tiny *enoteca* with excellent wines. For dinner, we head over to the Golden View, where we have requested a table by the window with Sasha as our waiter. A colorful, energetic character, he arrived 20 years ago from Serbia, escaping the Balkan war. Sasha completed university and came to Florence for vacation and he stayed.

We are seated at a small table by the window overlooking the Arno River, with a view of the Ponte Vecchio. Bill and I get sentimental, as this restaurant is directly across the river from our first apartment here 15 years ago.

Many of the best known cafes and restaurants have collected Bill's works. They are displayed prominently at places such as Trattoria Cammillo, Buco Poldo, Caffé Rivoire, L'Antico Noè and Vivoli. As Sister Wendy put it when she visited, "William, you became a great painter when you moved to Florence because you could finally focus all your energy in the pursuit of art." And, finally, I have completed my manuscript about our adventures in this Renaissance city.

We sit on our roof deck and gaze upon the Florentine skyline —the terra cotta rooftops and the always-breathtaking view of the Duomo, officially called the Cattedrale di Santa Maria del Fiore—Cathedral of Saint Mary of the Flower—in all its magnificence. It took 140 years to build, starting in 1296, and was finished in 1436; the dome engineered by Filippo Brunelleschi. That was 56 years before Columbus discovered America. It will still be here long after we are gone -- a humbling thought.

Florence has been our personal Renaissance. We are as committed to the city as we are to each other. The beauty of Florence and the reason we came and the reason we stayed endures.

Final Thoughts

The city is a cultural museum and does not change, but there have been notable changes in other areas, both for good and ill, over the past fifteen years:

*Dogs are still welcome inside trattorias and cafés. Owners have progressed to carrying plastic bags while walking their pets outside and picking up after them.

*The smoking ban in restaurants was a big success. Italy was the fourth country in the world to enact a nationwide smoke-free law. Since January 10, 2005, it is forbidden to smoke in all public indoor spaces, including bars, cafés, restaurants and discos.

*The new "Trashcube" may be one of the best inventions of the century for Florence. A neat, aboveground gray metal box with the Florentine emblem in red on the front is gradually replacing the archaic, massive, odorous dumpsters that dominated the streets of Florence. The new modules are usually found in orderly rows of four or six for recycling possibilities.

*The square around Santa Maria Novella is finally completed and is gorgeous, although it took an inordinate, or perhaps just an Italian, amount of time.

*Foreign students studying here (especially Americans) persist in drinking too much.

*Cobblestone streets and sidewalks are still treacherous for walking in narrow heeled shoes.

*As small shops give way to increased rent and are forced to go out of business, they are replaced by gelaterias. There are now too many and they are not all good. Vivoli is still the best.

*"Take out," *porta via,* once unheard of, is now accepted; restaurants and cafés have containers on hand.

*Select trattorias offer a gluten-free menu.

*The second floor of Mercato Centrale is no longer crammed with authentic fruit and vegetable stands. It is now completely modernized and houses several upscale cafés, as well as Eataly and Lorenzo de Medici's state-of-the-art cooking school.

*The American Express office on Via Dante Alghieri has long since been replaced by a Supermercato Metà.

*Sadly, Francesco did close Etrusca in Fiesole. Bill went to visit and a bank stands in place of what was our wonderful weekend retreat.

*New and obnoxious trends include tourists photographing their food. A meal is no longer for consumption and enjoyment; it is to be displayed on Facebook. I won't even elaborate on the "selfie" obsession.

* Everyone texts; security guards armed with machine guns stand lookout at the bank door texting. People walk down the street texting and not paying any attention to where they are going—an accident waiting to happen on these rocky roads and sidewalks.

*Street vendors hawk a new product every year. Last year was a palm-size glob with beady eyes in obnoxious iridescent colors of green, orange and blue. At most of the main tourist attractions, men would stand and throw it on a board on the ground. It would splat out and shrink back. Naturally, I bought a few for the grandkids. When I arrived at my daughter's house before Christmas, I gave one to her youngest son, age seven. He threw it on the hardwood kitchen floor with such force that it split open and started to ooze a noxious gel.

*Art educators and renowned artists Rose and Claire have moved house, studio, and school to a place called Poppiano in Tuscany. It took them 5 years to convert a former textile factory. They split their time between here and South Africa.

*Matteo Renzi, the city's young mayor from June 2009 to 2014, became Prime Minister of Italy at the age of 39, overtaking Benito Mussolini's record as the youngest person to become Prime Minister of Italy since unification in 1871.

*Perhaps the saddest change of all: Italian men no longer follow, ogle, pinch me or try to pick me up any more. Now, horrifyingly, I am treated with great respect; *"Buongiorno, Senora!"*

*When we began our journey we had no grandchildren. Now we are blessed with eleven.

Our Favorite Restaurants, Cafès, Trattorie, and other venues

Caffè Rivoire
Piazza della Signoria 50122 Firenze, Italy
+39 055 214412
www.rivoire.it

La Loggia Degli Albizi
Borgo Albizi, 39 Rosso, Firenze, Italy
+39 055 247 9574

Roberto Cavalli's Caffè Giacosa
Via della Spada, 1050123 Firenze, Italy
+39 055 2776328

Cantinetta di Verrazzano
Via dei Tavolini, 18/r 50122 Firenze, Italy
+39 055 268590

Trattoria Cammillo
Borgo San Jacopo, 57/r, 50125 Firenze, Italy
+39 055 212427

Trattoria del Carmine,
Piazza del Carmine 18, 50124 Firenze, Italy
+39 055 218601

Osteria L'Antico Noe'
Volta Di San Piero, 6r 50122 Firenze, Italy
+39 055 2340838
lanticonoe@libero.it

Ristorante Buca Poldo
Via Chiasso degli Armagnati, 2/r, Firenze, Italy
+39 055 2396578
www.bucapoldo.it/

Golden View Open Bar, Pizzeria-Ristorante
Via de Bardi, 58/r, 50125 Firenze, Italy
+39 055 214502
www.goldenviewopenbar.com

Trattoria Armando
Borgo Ognisanti 140/r, 50134 Firenze, Italy
+39 055 217263
www.trattoria-armando.com

Trattoria 13 Gobbi
Via del Porcellana 9/r, Firenze, Italy
+39 055 284015

Enoteca Le volpi e l'uva.
Piazza de' Rossi 1, 50125 Firenze, Italy
+39 055 2398132
www.levolpieluva.com

Alimentari Perini
Piazza del Mercato Centrale, 50123 Firenze, Italy
+39 055 2398306

Mercato di Sant'Ambrogio
Piazza Lorenzo Ghiberti, 50122 Firenze, Italy
Italymercato.ambrogio@virgilio.it

Macelleria Menoni Luca (butcher)
Int. Mercato di Sant'Ambrogio, Firenze, Italy
+39 055 2480778

Il Teatro del Sale
Via dè Macci, 118, 50122 Firenze, Italy
+39 055 200 14 92

Chiesa di Santa Margherita de' Cerchi (Dante Church)
Piazza dei Giuochi, 50122 Firenze, Italy

Zecchi Colori Belle Arti (Art Supplies)
Via dello Studio 19/r 50100 Firenze, Italy
+39 055 211470
zecchifi@tin.it

Circolo Golf Ugolino
Via Chiantigiana per Strada, 3, 50023
Impruneta, Firenze, Italy
+39 055 2301009
info@golfugolino.it

Pegna (specialty food store that delivers)
Via dello Studio, 8, 50122 Firenze, Italy
+39 055 282701

If you need to ship anything from Florence:
Mail Boxes Etc.
Via della Scala, 13, 50123 Firenze, Italy
+39 055 268173

Recipes

<u>Lisa's Basic Tomato Sauce for Pasta</u>
<u>Serves 8</u>

<u>I like to keep containers of this simple, classic</u>
<u>sauce in my freezer.</u>

2 28-ounce cans plum tomatoes
1 large yellow onion, peeled and thickly sliced
3 stalks celery, chopped
1 carrot, sliced
Large bunch basil
½ cup olive oil
1 teaspoon sugar
Salt, to taste
Freshly ground pepper, to taste

Put all ingredients in a large non-reactive pot. Cook over medium-low heat for 45 minutes, stirring occasionally. Remove from heat and let cool. When cool, put through a food mill. The sauce can be frozen.

Lisa's Veal Stew
Serves 6

This is a great company dish that can be made in advance. You can serve it with rice or noodles and a green salad.

2 tablespoons olive oil
2 tablespoons butter
2 pounds lean veal stew meat, cut in 1-inch cubes
Flour for dredging
3 pinches dried sage
1 cup white wine
1 beef bouillon cube
Salt, to taste
Freshly ground pepper

Heat olive oil and butter in a sauté pan over medium heat.

Dredge veal in flour and sauté until lightly browned.

Add dried sage, and cook for 30 seconds.

Turn up heat and add white wine, and cook until the wine evaporates.

Put enough water to cover the contents by at least 2 inches. Add bouillon cube.

Add salt and pepper to taste, being careful not to add too much salt. The bouillon cube is salty. Cook for one hour, simmering gently.

Lisa's Minestrone

This is another recipe that freezes well. I like to serve this hearty soup with fresh, crusty Tuscan bread.

¼ cup olive oil
1 large white onion, finely chopped
3-4 stalks celery, chopped
3 carrots, cut in thirds
½ pound green beans
4-5 potatoes, peeled and cut into1-inch cubes
4 small zucchini, chopped
1 bunch chard or Swiss chard
8 ounces dry white cannellini beans, soaked overnight and drained; or 8 ounces canned beans.
2 tablespoons tomato paste
Basil
½ teaspoon sage or one sage leaf
½ teaspoon rosemary or one sprig
½ teaspoon thyme or 2 sprigs
1 teaspoon oregano or 2 sprigs
1 beef bouillon cube
½ teaspoon sea salt
½ teaspoon freshly ground pepper

Heat the olive oil in a large pot over medium heat. Add the onion, celery, and carrot and cook about 15 minutes until the vegetables are soft, lowering the heat, if necessary, to prevent the onion from burning.

Add the green beans and the remaining ingredients and cover with two quarts water.

Cook covered for 2 hours. (If using canned beans, add at them just before serving.)

Tiramisu

A classic Italian dessert that is a rich and satisfying end to any meal.

10 ounces lady fingers
3 eggs
14 ounces mascarpone
4 tablespoons sugar
3 tablespoons brandy or rum
1 cup freshly brewed coffee
Unsweetened cocoa for dusting

Beat the egg yolks with the sugar in an electric mixer, then add the mascarpone, mixing to form a smooth cream.

Flavor with the brandy or rum. In a separate bowl, beat the egg whites until stiff and add them to the cream, folding them in gently from the bottom to the top.

Pour the coffee into a wide, deep dish, add as much sugar as you like, dilute with a few spoonfuls of water and a spoonful of brandy.

Dip the sponge fingers one at a time in the coffee and place a layer of these in a soufflé dish or a similar container with high sides. Spread half of the cream over the lady fingers and level the surface. Continue making layers in this way, finishing with a layer of cream.

Place the dessert in the refrigerator for at least 2 hours. Just before serving it, dust the top with unsweetened cocoa.

Maria's Salsa Amatriciana
This is a spicy sauce.

1 onion, finely chopped
¼ cup olive oil
1 dry pepperoncino
5 medium-thick slices or one solid 1 ¼-inch-thick piece, approximately 1/3 pound pancetta (smoked bacon), finely chopped.
1 28-ounce can peeled Italian tomatoes with their juice
Salt to taste

Saute the onion in olive oil. Add the pepperoncino and the pancetta or bacon. When the onions and bacon are browned, add the can of tomatoes and break them up with a wooden spoon. Cook, uncovered, on medium-low heat for 45 minutes, making sure the mixture doesn't dry out. If necessary, add water to thin the sauce. Add salt to taste. If you are using bacon, it may not need much.

Serve over your favorite pasta.

Maria's Polpette from Positano
These meatballs are light and irresistible served with Lisa's Tomato Sauce over spaghetti.

2 pounds prime ground beef
4 pieces of thin white bread with crusts (Pepperidge Farm, for example), soaked in milk
½ clove of garlic minced or chopped fine
One bunch Italian parsley leaves, chopped fine
1 cup freshly grated Parmigiano-Reggiano
3 eggs
Salt and freshly ground pepper to taste

Mix all ingredients together and form small balls.

Fry in ½ cup olive oil or peanut oil, turning frequently, until browned all over.

To serve: Add to your favorite tomato sauce, heat thoroughly, and serve over pasta of your choice.

Positano Posse Gateau of Potatoes
Serves 10

This flavorful dish can be served as a main course with a green salad or as part of a buffet. It also can be doubled or cut in half easily.

4 pounds peeled potatoes cut in chunks
4 ounces butter
6 ounces buffalo mozzarella
4 ounces Italian salami (not spicy), finely chopped
4 ounces cooked ham or proscuitto, shredded
4 ounces Parmigiano Reggiano, grated
Milk
Salt
Freshly ground pepper
3 eggs
Bread crumbs

Preheat oven to 375 degrees F.

Bring a pot of salted water to a boil. Add potatoes and cook until potatoes are cooked through (approximately 15 minutes). Put the potatoes in a large bowl and using a potato masher, mash them, adding the butter and enough milk to make a smooth mixture (being careful not to make the mixture too runny). Beat in one egg at a time.

Combine half the salami and half the ham and stir into the potato mixture. Then stir in the Parmesan cheese.

Butter a large casserole dish. Spread half the potato mixture in the dish.

Cover with the remaining salami.

Add a layer of mozzarella.

Top with the remaining ham.

Spread the remaining potato mixture over the ham.

Sprinkle with breadcrumbs.

Dot with butter and bake for one hour.

Serve hot or at room temperature.

Maria's Chicken Cutlets

Try these simple cutlets with pasta and peas sautéed with garlic and olive oil.

6 boneless, skinless chicken breasts cut into thin cutlets and pounded
1 ¼ cup unseasoned dry bread crumbs
Two extra-large eggs
1 teaspoon finely chopped parsley
1 teaspoon grated Parmigiano-Reggiano
½ clove of garlic, chopped very fine
¼ teaspoon pepper
dash of salt

Whisk together all ingredients, except chicken and bread crumbs, in a shallow bowl.

Place cutlets one at a time in bread crumb mixture. Turn over several times and pat with palm of hand till well coated. Place on a large platter or sheet pan.

Refrigerate a minimum of one hour.

In a large frying pan, add vegetable oil (not olive oil) and heat. When hot, add chicken cutlets and saute until golden brown.

Serve with Anchovy Butter
Softened stick of butter;

Anchovy paste from a tubeCombine butter and anchovy paste, to taste. Serve a teaspoon of the butter on each cutlet.

Authentic Bolognese from Bologna

I was given this recipe for "ragu" by our waiter at the renowned Ristorante Pappagallo (The Parrot) in Bologna. About 50 miles north of Florence, Bologna is as famous for its cuisine as it is for its miles of *portici,* or covered arcades. The high-speed train from Florence to Bologna takes just 36 minutes. Another art-filled city with Europe's oldest university, it is well worth a visit.

1 onion, finely chopped
¼ cup olive oil
1 carrot, finely chopped
1 stalk celery, finely chopped
2 pounds ground beef
¼ bottle, about 1 ½ cups, white wine
1 28-ounce can peeled Italian tomatoes with their juice
2 tablespoons butter
½ chicken bouillon cube

Saute onion in olive oil till soft. Add carrot and celery and continue to sauté (about 10 minutes).

Add beef and cook till browned. Add wine, tomatoes, and chicken bouillon and cook over low heat, uncovered, for 3 hours. Add a little water or more wine if the sauce is becoming too dry.

Add 2 tablespoons of butter and mix into the sauce thoroughly.

Serve over tagliatelle, a ribbon-like pasta. Italian chefs insist that the meat clings better to a flatter pasta shape.

Insalata di Zucchini

A salad of zucchini with the luxurious touch of truffle oil. It makes an elegant first course for a dinner party.

½ pound fresh arugula (3 large bunches)
1 1 ¾ ounce jar pignoli (pine nuts)
Paper-thin slices of zucchini, sliced with a vegetable peeler--six per serving
½ cup truffle oil
¼ teaspoon freshly ground black pepper
Parmesan cheese, for serving

If the arugula has roots attached, cut them off. Wash with cold water and dry the leaves in a salad spinner. Place arugula on individual plates.

Sprinkle arugula with enough truffle oil to moisten the leaves.

Fold back the zucchini slices and arrange over the arugula so it looks like a flower.

Place a tablespoon of pine nuts in the center of the salad and sprinkle with pepper.

Drizzle with more truffle oil.

Shave Parmesan into shards and scatter on top.

A Note About the Author

Susan Kelley is the author of five nonfiction books: *REAL WOMEN SEND FLOWERS, WHY MEN COMMIT, WHY MEN STRAY/WHY MEN STAY,THE SECOND TIME AROUND: Everything You Need to Know to Make Your Remarriage Happy* and *I OPRAHED, And Other Adventures of a Woman of a Certain Age.* Her best-selling relationship books have been translated into several foreign languages, including Japanese, Polish, and Dutch.

Susan has appeared as guest "relationship expert" on *The Oprah Winfrey Show, The Early Show* on CBS NEWS, MSNBC, Fox TV, and numerous other national and local television programs. In addition to her career as a writer, Kelley has forty-five years of experience as a professional model and actress, which serves her well as she travels to publicize her books. She is a member of SAG, AFTRA, the Authors Guild, and the Writers Guild of America, East.

She lives in Florence, Italy, and Sarasota, Florida.

Made in the USA
Lexington, KY
02 January 2016